TITANIC
Legacy

TITANIC Legacy

Disaster as Media Event and Myth

Paul Heyer

PRAEGER

Westport, Connecticut
London

Library of Congress Cataloging-in-Publication Data

Heyer, Paul.
  Titanic legacy : disaster as media event and myth / Paul Heyer.
    p. cm.
  Includes bibliographical references and index.
  ISBN 0–275–95352–1 (alk. paper)
  1. Titanic (Steamship). 2. Shipwrecks—North Atlantic Ocean.
  I. Title.
  G530.T6H49 1995
  363.12'3'09631—dc20   95–22016

HEY

British Library Cataloguing in Publication Data is available.

Library of Congress Catalog Card Number: 95–22016
ISBN: 0–275–95352–1

First published in 1995

Praeger Publishers, 88 Post Road West, Westport, CT 06881
An imprint of Greenwood Publishing Group, Inc.

Printed in the United States of America

∞™

The paper used in this book complies with the
Permanent Paper Standard issued by the National
Information Standards Organization (Z39.48–1984).

10 9 8 7 6 5 4 3

To the memory of Elaine Sylvestre Heyer,
who first told me about the event
and its enduring lessons.

And, behold, I, even I, do bring a flood of waters upon the earth, to destroy all flesh, wherein is the breath of life, from under heaven; *and* everything that is the earth shall die.

—Genesis 6:1

Now small fowls flew screaming over the great yawning gulf; a sullen white surf beat against its steep sides; then all collapsed and the great shroud of the sea rolled on as it rolled five thousand years ago.

—Herman Melville, *Moby Dick*

Contents

Photographs follow page 101.

Preface

The sinking of the *Titanic* is our century's first collective nightmare. The confused and anguished response it provoked—culture shock is the term that comes to mind—can be seen as a harbinger of reactions that would follow Hiroshima, the Holocaust, JFK's assassination, and most recently, the Oklahoma City bombing.

Since the bewildering events of 1912, the ship has never strayed far from media concern. In 1985, the discovery of the wreck attracted worldwide attention. A year later, the *Challenger* explosion repeated the *Titanic's* lesson of technological hubris. Most recently, the nineties are experiencing a new surge of interest in response to the release of the giant-screen IMAX film, *Titanica*, and the controversy surrounding the sale and exhibition of the salvaged artifacts. As fin-de-siècle and end of millennium anxiety begins to grip us, it seems we cannot let the great ship rest in peace . . . nor she us.

Many commentaries have been written about the *Titanic* disaster. Most deal with what happened, why, and all the "what ifs" that will forever cling to it. My concern here is not to provide another such chronicle, nor is it about the lives of those involved. What I do address are the implications of the event—the legacy the ship's demise imparted to a world that has still not fully recovered from it. More than just a tragedy entailing great loss of life, the sinking of the *Titanic* endures as our century's most persistent reminder of the danger in underestimating nature and overestimating technology.

My interest in the consequences of this disaster derives from an encounter between a childhood fascination, inspired by films such as *Titanic* and *A Night To Remember,* and a career writing and teaching about mass media. They converged unexpectedly during the 1980s, when I joined countless others enthralled by press and television coverage of the search for the wreck. This prompted a desire to research aspects of the disaster, particularly its influence over a variety of communication media, and media's role in immortalizing the story.

In organizing the diverse array of information pertaining to the *Titanic* and the media, I have adopted a fourfold plan. Part 1 begins with an overview of the persistent relationship between the *Titanic* and twentieth century communications and continues with a look at the circumstances that brought the concept of such large liners into being.

Part 2 deals with the *Titanic* in the context of the prebroadcasting era of radio. My concern is with the way the disaster dramatized the enormous potential—and limitations—of Macroni's wireless telegraph. This entails looking at how the sinking hastened the passage of new and precedent-setting regulations governing the medium's operation.

Press coverage is the subject of Part 3. Discounting war reportage, the sinking of the *Titanic* is one of the biggest single-event news stories of this century, second perhaps only to JFK's assassination. Every news-gathering technique was employed, new ones were devised for the occasion, and journalistic ethics were pushed to their limits. This scenario is examined, along with the fortunes of *The New York Times*, the paper that benefited most from the tragedy.

Part 4 looks at the representation of the *Titanic* in popular culture since 1912: how, in print media and in film, her voyage has made the transition from a disaster steeped in mystery to a moral tale of mythic proportions. Assessing this transformation evokes a comparison with literary archetypes, from Genesis to science fiction. And here, as in most of the preceding chapters, it is not just the fate of the *Titanic* that I want to reflect on, but the meanings it has generated.

Throughout the research and writing of this book I found support everywhere I turned. It is inconceivable that the project could have been undertaken without the assistance of the Titanic Historical Society (THS), located in Indian Orchard, Massachusetts. The THS is a treasure trove, and their quarterly magazine, the *Titanic Commutator*, is of incalculable value to anyone interested in the great ship and her era. THS president, Edward Kamuda, graciously took time to answer my initial correspondence and helped me secure difficult-to-find material. I also wish to thank *Titanic* archivists John Booth and Sean Coughlan, and historian Stephen Kern for kindly agreeing to read portions of the initial manuscript. My research assistant, Karen Wall, has been an invaluable source of information and inspiration. Responsibility, however, for any inaccurate interpretations or overstated conclusions is solely mine.

My *Titanic* odyssey has led me many places, from the New York Public Library—may the powers that be grant that venerable institution longer operating hours—to small museums in rural Australia. Whenever I publicly presented aspects of the project, response was enthusiastic, whether the context was the broadcast media, CBC (Canada), and ABC (Australia), or an academic one. In the last category, I wish to thank communication and media studies departments at Simon Fraser, McGill, and Concordia Universities in Canada, and the University of Western Sydney, Nepean, Australia.

Although a list of the many individuals who encouraged me along the way would be too lengthy to cite here, special thanks are due: Bob Anderson, Natollie Bardell, Alison Beale, Anouk Bélanger, Pierre Bélanger, Judy Bell, Bill Buxton, Ian Chunn, Hart Cohen, Leonie Crichly, David Crowley, Dominique Darmon, Ian Dyck, Robert Epp, Bill Ewing, Gail Faurschou, Jib Fowles, Robin Fox, Steve Gouthro, Terry Guthridge, Dale Hannay, John Harris, Amir and Salah Hassanpour, Pat Hindley, Lynne Hissey, Harry Irwin, Sut Jhaly, Yasmin Jiwani, Lisa and Ray Knowles, Lisa Kofod, Brian Lewis, Carol Liston, Rolly Lorimer, Don Lynch, Mary Malins, Garry McCarron, Lianne McLarty, Ken McQueen, Trish Marshall, Lucie Menkveld, Vanneau and Sacha Neesham, Virginia Nightingale, Barbara Oborska, Lise Ouimet, Richard Pinet, Andrew Preston, Firoozeh Radjai, Gertrude Robinson, Lorna Roth, Ann Kristin Salbuvik, Reana Selody-Joubert, Neena Shahani, Brian Shoesmith, Ray Straatsma, Mark Thornton, Lionel Tiger, Heather Trexler-Remoff, Robert Walker, Karen Wall, Gretchen and Julian Weaver, Tony Wilden, Jery Zaslove, Denyse Zenner, and Ania Zofia.

Working again with the Greenwood Publishing Group, this time with their Praeger imprint, has been an eminently rewarding experience. I wish to thank my editor, Nina Pearlstein, for her patience, support, and impeccable judgment, and Maureen Melino and Emily Okenquist who, with skill and foresight, navigated the manuscript through production.

Part I

INTRODUCTION

A ship is a habitat before being a means of transport.
—Roland Barthes, *Mythologies*

It is Sunday, 14 April 1912, 400 miles southeast of the coast of New-foundland in space, 11:40 P.M. in time. The North Atlantic sits dark and motionless, like a great pool of oil. The air is as cold and sharp as a razor. In seconds, the renowned creation of an era is going to collide with an anonymous fragment of nature.

And so it began. Although it is not my concern to provide a detailed assessment of the event, relevant facts pertaining to it will inevitably emerge in subsequent discussions. The reader, however, might benefit at the outset from the following brief summary of what happened and when.

On 10 April 1912, the *Titanic* set sail on her maiden voyage from Southampton, England, to New York, where she was due to arrive on 16 April. She was the largest liner ever built, 882 feet in length, 92 feet wide, and 46,328 tons in weight. Prior to the collision, the ship had been steaming at her fastest speed of the voyage, 22½ knots, into a region where several reports had warned of the presence of ice. When the look-out spotted the iceberg, at perhaps 500 yards, it was too late to do more than just begin evasive maneuvers.

Most on board felt the collision as a mild shudder and were unper-turbed. What resulted was a glancing blow that cut a 300-foot slit below the water line toward the bow on the starboard side. Five or six watertight compartments were breached (perhaps semiwatertight would have been a better term, since they did not extend all the way to the top deck). The ship could only stay afloat if up to four were flooded—this led to later speculation that a head-on led collision might have been preferable. The flooding compartments gradually pulled the ship down by the bow. She vanished at 2:20 A.M.

There were 2,227 passengers and crew on board; 705 survived in 20 lifeboats. The number of lifeboats was inadequate because of a British Board of Trade regulation that based the number of lifeboats a ship carried on her tonnage, not on the number of passengers; nevertheless, the available lifeboats could have held 1,200 people. Shortly after the collision the wireless operator began sending an SOS, followed by the ship's position. Morse lamp was also used when a nearby ship, possibly the *Californian,* came into view, and signal rockets were sent up. The first ship on the scene was the Cunard liner *Carpathia.* She arrived shortly after 4 A.M., having been fifty-eight miles away when she first picked up the *Titanic's* SOS. The *Carpathia* took the survivors to New York. They arrived on the evening of 18 April.

On 19 April a committee of the United States Senate chaired by William Alden Smith began an inquiry into the causes of the disaster. It released its report on 28 May. The document was critical of established maritime practice in the North Atlantic; the comportment of the *Titanic's* parent company, the White Star Line, before, during, and after the disaster; and the captain of the *Californian,* Stanley Lord, for not responding to the *Titanic's* signal rockets. The committee was not empowered to lay charges, but its findings had a major influence on subsequent regulatory policy regarding shipping and wireless use.

On 2 May, a British Board of Trade inquiry was launched. It was led by a judge, Lord Mersey, and released its report on 30 July. This inquiry was more technically minded than the American effort. It was also less critical of established maritime practice and not as severe in its condemnation of the White Star Line; however, the position taken on the *Californian* and her captain paralleled the American judgment. Numerous commentators, then and now, have argued that the British inquiry was a "whitewash" that protected both the Board of Trade and White Star from the severe censure they should have received. No charges were laid, although the inquiry was empowered to do so, but a number of regulations were changed, most immediately the one pertaining to the number of lifeboats required on a ship.

1

The Persistent Disaster

Since the startling events of April 1912, the *Titanic* has been the subject of a seemingly endless flow of commentary and reflection. The list includes everything from survivors' accounts and formal studies to novels, poems, plays, musical compositions, a half-dozen feature films, numerous television specials, several associations dedicated to preserving her legacy, and frequent reference to the ship in the informal discourses of everyday life. The most recent chapter in this ongoing phenomenon began with the discovery of the wreck in September 1985 by a joint American and French expedition headed by Robert Ballard.

Finding the *Titanic* has not resolved the mystery surrounding her demise or diminished interest in it. Quite the opposite, as post-1985 media coverage attests. The last time such fascination occurred was four decades ago, when Walter Lord's best selling account, *A Night to Remember* (1955), was published and eventually made into a movie in 1958. But this time interest in the *Titanic* shows no sign of waning. Perhaps a reflexive spirit prompted by the century and the millennium drawing to a close is responsible, coupled with the influence of a more recent disaster, which has suggested that the lessons of history are sometimes repeated for the benefit of those who did not pay close enough attention the first time.

In January 1986, the space shuttle *Challenger* exploded shortly after liftoff. This incident led many to rethink what had occurred seventy-four years earlier. Several parallels are striking: new technology overextended; the death of an identifiable cross-section of humanity; a disappearance into the North Atlantic; the possibility that ice was a factor in the failure of the *Challenger's* O rings; and the tantalizing list of "what ifs" that still surround both tragedies. Less well known is the role of Robert Ballard's underwater search vehicle *Argo*, which was used to look for both the *Titanic* and *Challenger*. Nevertheless, the moral lessons and mythical potential of the *Challenger* remain limited by its recentness. We remember it more as a news story than as history. Although the *Challenger* continues to be overshadowed by the *Titanic*, it is possible that as the twenty-first century puts increasing emphasis on the "final frontier" of space exploration, the space shuttle's demise might become the more metaphorically relevant event.

The latest barrage of media commentary regarding the *Titanic* has been both frivolous and serious. On the lighter side, she has surfaced in scenes from *Time Bandits* and *Ghostbusters II* and been the subject of several tabloid headlines claiming the discovery of survivors who came through a time-warp. In a more sobering vein were newspaper articles covering the 1992 British inquiry to assess the "*Californian* Incident"—it was this ship, captained by the much criticized Stanley Lord, that was allegedly within view of the *Titanic* and did not respond to her distress calls.

Also of note is *Titanica*, the giant-screen IMAX film of the wreck, released in appropriate venues around the world in 1993. It has inspired wonder and raised old and new questions, as has the controversy surrounding artifacts brought up in 1987 by the French codiscoverers of the wreck and in 1993 by a New York–based company, RMS Titanic, Inc. Although legal within the context of international law, these actions have been widely condemned. After the French expedition, the United States passed legislation to prohibit, within its borders, the trade or exhibition for profit of any recovered pieces. Antisalvage lobbyists argue that the remains of the *Titanic* should be declared either an international grave or a restricted archeological site. No other wreck can claim the former status, and none dating from this century, the latter. The passions aroused by this incident suggest the *Titanic* now possesses an aura similar to a classical ruin or a religious shrine.

Somewhere between the frivolous and the serious was the television special that aired 28 October 1988, "Return to the *Titanic* . . . Live!" The opening of a recovered safe was to provide the climactic moment. The program merits commentary because of the way it raised (or lowered), along with the accompanying media hype, the story of the *Titanic* to an extraordinary level of public visibility. Not since the discovery of the wreck three years earlier had the ship been deluged with such coverage.

This telecast belongs to a genre sometimes referred to as a pseudoevent: a news story created especially for the media. On such occasions the audience is supposed to experience the "revelation" along with, not after, the attendant experts. The mystery of the *Titanic* was presented as a kind of deep sea striptease: aspects of the saga were told with the safe lurking tantalizingly in the background. The host, Telly Savalas, conveyed sincerity, but he seemed haggard, missed several cues, and at one point almost tripped over a chair—an understandable situation given that the broadcast originated live from Paris in the early morning hours to coincide with North American prime time. The *Titanic's* story, however, could not but overwhelm and make anticlimactic whatever the safe might reveal, which in this case was some soggy bank notes and a handful of memorabilia. Later allegations of fraud—it was claimed the safe had been opened beforehand—kept what had transpired newsworthy for nearly a week. The press had a field day criticizing television's attempt to create live news.

Although this broadcast has been largely forgotten, the *Titanic* can still garner headlines when some new aspect of her story is revealed. One reason is that ever since the emergence of modern mass communications just over a century ago, a close relationship has come to exist between them and major disasters. During such times, these conduits of information achieve peak prominence, strongly shaping public reaction and opinion. But the event being communicated also influences the medium involved. Throughout the twentieth century a series of disasters, in which the sinking of the *Titanic* holds a prominent place, have highlighted and transformed the potential of a variety of media. The first example is the San Francisco earthquake of 1906.

Reaction to this event was more pronounced and widespread than would have been the case a generation earlier, a result of the new mass journalism pioneered by Joseph Pulitzer and William Randolph Hearst in the last decades of the nineteenth century. Coverage was also influenced by an emerging series of transcontinental telephone linkups, which increased the information flow beyond what would have been possible using the telegraph alone. The extensive use of both media in this reportage set a precedent for future news gathering, one that the *Titanic* would extend to an international stage by adding wireless to the repertoire of journalistic tools. And, in a case of historical "aftershock," the 1989 San Francisco earthquake became a major television spectacle. Networks scrambled for definitive coverage using their resources to the fullest.

During the 1930s, the power and credibility of the mass circulation newspaper, which had already played a prominent role in the public's perception of disasters such as the *Titanic*, was challenged by radio's ability to deliver news more rapidly and, at times, live. An example of this new journalism of the airwaves was chillingly demonstrated in the 1937 broadcast of the crash of the *Hindenberg* in Lakehurst, New Jersey. Many accounts cite this as a live transmission, but it aired on 7 May, the day after the hydrogen-filled dirigible was consumed in flames. The media consequences were nonetheless telling: print journalism had a serious rival.

A year later, radio's potential to capture events "as they happened" was realistically incorporated into Orson Welles's legendary presentation of H.G. Wells's *War of the Worlds*. This story of a Martian invasion created a major panic. Both Welles and the network (CBS) were severely criticized, thus creating an opportunity for many newspapers to chastise their rival medium for overreaching itself. Nevertheless, the program and its aftermath did not impede the ascendancy of radio, which peaked with coverage of the events of World War II. The resonant voice of Edward R. Murrow broadcasting from London kept millions of North Americans riveted to their sets. Welles eventually went on to a distinguished career as a film director and actor. One of his last projects, completed in 1984, only a year before he died, was as narrator of, *The Search for the* Titanic, a documentary film about an unsuccessful attempt to locate the wreck undertaken by Texas oil millionaire Jack Grimm; the film was also unsuccessful.

In the postwar years, radio's primacy as a source for late-breaking news was gradually challenged by television, and here, also, tragedy, conflict, and disaster have played significant roles. Key events include the assassination of President Kennedy, the Vietnam War, the *Challenger* explosion, and, more recently, the Gulf War, the crisis in the Balkans, and the Oklahoma City bombing. However, in the case of the Gulf War, television coverage suffered from a lack of visuals and was often no better than what radio offered—some argue it was worse, because of the way several inaccurate and misleading images were used to exploit the situation.

Where does the sinking of the *Titanic* fit with respect to these developments? In various ways, it relates to all the media previously mentioned. Her initial circumstances were brought to public awareness through a dynamic web of information movement whose strands included the telegraph, telephone, wireless, and popular press. Her fate has been dramatized and analyzed on radio and television and in film.

The story of the *Titanic* also presents us with elements that are more difficult to assess—and access. In addition to being one of this century's major news stories, it has become a mystery and a myth of unparalleled enormity. It remains a mystery how and why, at almost full speed on the clearest of evenings, the "unsinkable" *Titanic* met the iceberg that authored its doom; as myth, the *Titanic* shares with the *Challenger* the capacity to derive a moral lesson from technological failure.

Why are we so fascinated by a disaster that throughout our century has been frequently surpassed by others in terms of loss of life? Partial explanations have been occasionally attempted. Most deal with the moral implications of the story—technological arrogance leading to a disregard for the forces of nature, the rich and famous paying with their lives, and the disaster as a finale for one era and overture to the next.

Explaining the meaning of the *Titanic*, however, entails not just analyzing the way her fate evokes literary notions of the tragic. It necessitates appraising the cultural and technological circumstances in which the drama has been, and is still being, played out. Using what can perhaps be described as the "archival archaeology" of a variety of media, we can then begin the task of unraveling the *Titanic*'s greatest mystery and central theme of subsequent chapters: not why she struck an iceberg on a cold April night once-upon-a-time, but the hold the event still has over us.

2

Realizing a Dream, Anticipating a Nightmare

In the eighteenth century, that eminently quotable man of letters, Dr. Samuel Johnson, was once asked what he thought about sea travel. He likened it to "being in jail with the chance of being drowned." By the early years of the twentieth century, the odds of being drowned while on an ocean voyage had diminished considerably, and even third-class ("steerage") accommodations were a substantial improvement over most prisons. First-class passengers could travel in a state of nirvana unthinkable only a generation earlier.

During the 1950s, the Cunard Line, facing competition from the airlines that would soon end the glory days of ocean travel between Europe and North America, coined the slogan: "Getting there is half the fun." It would have been just as appropriate in 1912 as a lure for travel on the jewels of Cunard's fleet, the *Lusitania* and *Mauretania*. Even then competition was severe. Cunard's main rival was the White Star Line, which could offer the *Olympic* and, for at least one voyage, her sister ship the *Titanic*. These vessels, especially the *Titanic*, had appointments so sumptuous that today's advertising hype might promote them with the phrase, "Getting there is all the fun."

Both companies had continental challengers, most notably Bremen's North German Lloyd and the Hamburg-Amerika Line, or HAPAG (Hamburg-Amerikanische Packetfahrt Actien-Gesellschaft). The paying customer could choose to travel either a little bit faster (Cunard/North German Lloyd) or with a touch more luxury (White Star/HAPAG), or simply according to a convenient time and place of departure. It was as if there was a conscious attempt to push behind the historical horizon all memories of those dank and uncertain crossings that had so often plagued previous centuries' ocean travel.

While White Star, Cunard, and their German rivals strove for a new standard of comfort and speed in ocean travel, a high priority was also placed on precise and reliable schedules. Previously, the model for temporal consistency had been the railways. Shipping timetables, in contrast, had been traditionally subject to the vicissitudes of the North Atlantic, and during much of the nineteenth century they were "guesstimates" at best. In the days of sail, arrival times could be off by as much as several weeks. Early steamers, although not as tyrannized by the weather, were nonetheless affected by it.

Up until the 1890s, or only about a decade prior to the planning of the *Titanic*, virtually all transatlantic liners carried auxiliary sailing gear; ironically, earlier in the century it had been the steam engines that were considered auxiliary. The sail rigging could be deployed in the case of engine failure or to conserve fuel by taking advantage of exceptionally favorable winds. When a ship was late during the nineteenth century, weather was usually assumed to be the culprit, with mechanical breakdown an additional possibility if the ship was a steamer. After about one week's delay, serious thoughts might be entertained regarding the possibility of a disaster.

To implement what had been a long cherished dream—a transatlantic schedule based on same-day weekly departures—White Star conceived the *Titanic* as part of a triumverate. Her sister ships were the *Olympic,* launched in 1911, and the *Britannic,* launched in 1915. Three ships were necessary for the service, given a five-to-six-day travel period and layovers that might last as long as a week. The *Titanic's* demise thwarted the company's attempt to be first with this transatlantic shuttle operation, but they would have been beaten by Cunard in any case. In 1914 the *Aquitania* joined the *Lusitania* and *Mauretania* in finally achieving the impressive breakthrough.

Cunard had tried to accomplish the feat several years earlier by teaming the *Campania* with the *Lusitania* and *Mauretania,* but the plan was ill advised. The *Campania,* built in 1893, was an old-style, twin-screw steamer that simply could not weather the weather like her larger, turbine-driven half-sisters. It soon became apparent that for consistent travel time and ease of maintenance, three well-matched ships were required for reliable weekly departures.

These ambitious plans seem all the more so when we consider how rapid were the transformations that made them possible. In the 1850s—a time when steam auxilliary engines and iron ships were just exiting their prototypic phases—the overwhelming majority of crossings still took place in wooden sailing vessels. Under optimum conditions, the trip could be done in five weeks. The sanitary facilities, food, and quarters left much to be desired. By 1901, passage on the *Campania, Kaiser Wilhelm II,* or *Celtic* had reduced the time to five-and-half days, and even third-class accommodations included fresh meals, clean (if crowded) quarters, and decent sanitary facilities, assuming individuals had the patience to wait their turn. Several memoirs exist written by people who traveled as passengers in both eras. These accounts tend not to romanticize the days of sail.

More recently, travelers in our jet age who remember crossing the Atlantic in the 1950s during the last golden age of the great liners, perhaps on either of the two Queens or the SS *United States,* rarely hesitate to speak of the experience with nostalgia. Time lost by choosing sea over air, or gained vice versa, rarely seems significant in later life. Air travel tends to be forgettable, unless something goes wrong; ocean voyages are almost always memorable. When a contemporary airline uses the by-now generic motto, "The only way to fly," the phrase bespeaks confident succession from a time when flying was not the only way.

Nevertheless, ocean travel persists. The steady growth of the cruise ship industry indicates that a mode of transportation need not be thought of solely as a means to get from point A to point B. Such voyages have become, at best, pleasant parodies, theme parks citing an era that looms larger in our historical rear-view mirror the closer we come to our own fin-de-siècle. As the great maverick American economist and social theorist Thorstein Veblen prophetically noted almost one hundred years ago, when modern technological capacities render obsolete what was once a widespread and essential activity, the activity often resurfaces as a pasttime for leisure or amusement.

The first steam-assisted crossing of the Atlantic began with the *Savannah* in 1819. She was steam assisted at least during those highly visible and newsworthy moments of departure and arrival—media events are not solely a twentieth-century phenomenon. The available paddle-wheel technology was bulky. It consumed so much fuel that the modest gain in speed—it took four weeks to cross—was offset by diminished space and a ticket price limited to the affluent, who would also have to possess a degree of courage to risk their lives in such an unproven vessel. By 1838, ships such as the *Great Western* were using paddle wheels to reduce the crossing time to two weeks, with most of the voyage under steam rather than sail. Passenger space, however, was limited to eighty, with enough soot to cover everyone.

By the next decade, two developments helped improve both space and speed: the switch from paddle wheels to screw propellers and the use of iron in a ship's construction. In 1843, the *Great Britain* became the first vessel to employ both. Understandably, there were reservations regarding the use of iron, especially as to its buoyancy relative to wood. But as the new generation of ship engineers pointed out time and again, an iron ship is not only stronger, it is also lighter than a wooden one of the same dimensions because it does not have to be as thick in either the hull or beam. This consequent lightness aids speed. Also, wooden ships, laden as they were with iron and brass fittings, were not renowned for their floatation capacity when breached.

Cunard, which started service in 1840, had by the end of the decade become *the* success story of the passenger ship industry. Reliability and an exemplary safety record were the primary reasons. What an American challenger, Collins, offered in response was speed. In 1852 this dream of speed led to the Collins liner *Pacific* pushing down the time to cross to just under ten days. But in 1856 they also offered something else, a navigation lesson that in 1912 the *Titanic* seemed to have forgotten: the *Pacific* entered an ice field and vanished. Two years earlier her sister ship, the *Arctic,* had foundered after colliding with another vessel off Cape Race Newfoundland. In 1858, after only eight years of service, the Collins Line itself went the route of its two prized vessels.

The Collins ships had not only offered speed but also contained hitherto untried luxuries, such as large cabins, steam heating, and an ornate decor; some of these frills, however, were packed away as the ships would leave port so as not to be damaged by rough seas or seasick passengers.

The idea of outfitting a ship in the manner of an elegant hotel would be a precedent very much on the minds of the builders of the *Titanic,* but it did not have to wait till the Gilded Age for further elaboration. In 1858, after four years in the building, the *Great Eastern* was launched into the Thames. She was the most ambitious ship, relative to her time, that had ever been or probably ever will be conceived. Her near-19,000 tons made her five times larger than any previous vessel and would not be exceeded until the completion of the *Celtic* and *Kaiser Wilhelm II* in 1901. In contrast, the *Olympic* and *Titanic* surpassed the gross tonnage of the previous largest vessels of their era, the *Mauretania* and *Lusitania,* by a factor of "only" 50 percent. At almost 700 feet from stem to stern, the *Great Eastern* would not be nosed out in the length category until the *Oceanic II* entered service in 1899.

The *Great Eastern* was to have been called the *Leviathan.* The name "Titanic" would have been just as appropriate. Although the infamous *Titanic* was 200 feet longer, the *Great Eastern* was designed to carry 800 more passengers, giving her a maximum capacity of 4,000—or up to 10,000 as a troop ship. The audaciousness of the vessel was not approached until 1907, when White Star and the shipbuilder Harland and Wolff drafted plans for the *Olympic, Titanic,* and *Britannic.* It is not certain whether those involved in this project studied the history of the *Great Eastern* when so engaged. If not they should have. Lessons both positive and negative could have been gleaned.

Isambord Kingdom Brunel was the *Great Eastern*'s creator, a renowned civil engineer whose bridges and railways crisscrossed Britain. His previous venture in ship design had yielded the successful *Great Western*. Brunel conceived the *Great Eastern* as a combination paddle wheel and screw-driven vessel with a fifteen knots cruising speed. She also had the obligatory sail rigging: six masts, five of which were of sheet iron and doubled as funnels. Add to this a complement of five large funnels, or one more than the *Titanic*. The ship cut an awesome figure at the time and by the standards of any subsequent era.

As would be the case with the *Titanic*, the builders of the *Great Eastern* declared her "practically unsinkable." In the case of the *Great Eastern* this was closer to the truth. She had a double hull from waterline to keel—the *Titanic* only had a double bottom—with 2 feet 6 inches between the platings. Shortly after the *Titanic* sank, maritime historian Adam Kirkaldy noted that had her hull been designed along the lines of the *Great Eastern*'s, she might have survived the gash the iceberg imparted just below her waterline. (After the *Titanic* demise, the *Olympic* was, to use a contemporary term, "recalled" and fitted with an extended double skin similar to the one that graced her midcentury precursor.) The *Great Eastern*, like the *Titanic*, had her structure severely tested. In 1862, en route from Liverpool to New York, the ship struck a submerged rock off the coast of Long Island and the outer hull was breeched. Although she did not founder, the cost of repairs bankrupted the owners, and in 1864 they consigned the ship to the auction block.

The *Great Eastern* was not simply ahead of her time, or even at the leading edge, as was the *Titanic*, but completely outside it. Conceived in 1851 as the "Floating City" or "Crystal Palace of the sea" (after the famous Crystal Palace Exposition in London the same year), it was hoped she would turn large profits on the eastward run to Australia and points between. Her prodigious fuel capacity seemed to favor such long voyages, but her equally prodigious appetite for fuel consumption made operating her expensive. At every step of the *Great Eastern*'s brief history she was beset with problems: the launch took almost three months and resulted in several deaths, a rash of injuries, and the destruction of expensive equipment; the maiden voyage attracted only fifty-five paying customers; and in her final days of service, during the 1870s laying submarine telegraph cable, she lacked the maneuverability to make this a permanent métier. The list goes on, and when tallied, yields one of the nineteenth century's most notorious white elephants.

Like the *Titanic* and *Olympic*, the *Great Eastern* was appointed with lavish state rooms, lounges, and dining areas. These features, along with the luxurious upholstery and teak and walnut decor, were unlike anything yet seen on a ship and were harbingers of what the Gilded Age would eventually bring to maritime travel. Another link with the later Olympic class liners was rhe *Great Eastern*'s bulkiness and slow response to the helm. Several near misses at sea and a few wrecked wharves were the result. In the case of the White Star Line's dream machines, the deficiencies led to the *Olympic*'s collision with the *Hawke* in 1911—both ships made it back to port for repair—and the *Titanic* pulling the liner *New York* loose from her moorings as the former was leaving Southampton, resulting in an ominous near miss. It has also been claimed that had the *Titanic* been equipped with a rudder more commensurate with her size, she might have been able to steer clear of the iceberg.

When it came to general seaworthiness, however, the *Great Eastern* was clearly inferior to her giant successors. Storms were not merely an inconvenience; they tended to dislodge fixtures, flood staterooms, and make life miserable for those on board.

Ironically, the *Great Eastern*'s career ended as it began, dockside, with paid sightseeing excursions. In 1886, the ship that was inspired by the London Exposition of 1851 became part of the Liverpool Exposition and attracted a half million paying customers. A year later she was sold for scrap and perhaps demonstrated a modicum of revenge on her detractors when she proved to be extraordinarily difficult to break up.

Despite the failure of the *Great Eastern* to be a viable leap forward in size, comfort, and speed, the trend in this direction persisted, albeit in a less quantum fashion. Success in the competitive shipping business often meant knowing how far previous standards could be exceeded while still maintaining the public's confidence. Thomas Henry Ismay understood this formula when he entered the shipping business in 1867. Two years later, with financial backing from Gustavus Schwabe, a Hamburg investor, he organized the Oceanic Steam Navigation Company and purchased a small line known as White Star.

White Star's flagship, the *Royal Standard*, had regularly transported immigrants and cargo to Australia. Unfortunately, the company's record carried one noteworthy blemish that occurred in April of 1863 and that can be seen as an eerie harbinger of April 1912. Sailing east across the South Pacific on the homeward journey, the *Royal Standard* struck an iceberg. The damage was severe but, unlike the Collins liner, *Pacific,* the ship survived. Several anxious weeks were spent completing the crossing before she made port in Rio de Janeiro for repairs.

Ismay was soon convinced by Schwabe that greater economic possibilities lay in the North American run. The United States and Canada were teeming with raw materials such as wheat, timber, minerals, cotton, and tobacco. Anglo-America also had a large number of former immigrants and their first generation offspring, all anxious for a look at the place of their cultural origins. Travel in the other direction seemed assured. The dynamism of the New World provided an ongoing lure for a new generation of Europeans contemplating emigration. Ismay's vision was to commission ships large enough to handle comfortably this traffic and then to endow them with the type of luxury appointments that would attract an elite cadre of high-paying first-class passengers from both continents.

Under the management of Ismay, along with his partner William Imrie, the company began its new steamer service in 1871. Their flagship was the just completed *Oceanic*. She was 420 feet in length, weighed 38,000 tons, and had the capacity to make the crossing in just under 10 days. The *Oceanic* was slightly larger than the Cunard liners and almost as fast. Where she had a decided edge was in the domain of luxury appointments. Her large Grand Saloon and Great Parlor had spectacular high ceilings, were located amidships rather than aft (at the rear), and ran the entire width of the ship. The innovative location significantly reduced engine vibration and roll. There were also fireplaces with marble mantles and plush staterooms equipped with water taps and oil lamps. Such ostentation was not without risk, since comparisons with the *Great Eastern* would be inevitable. Although the *Oceanic* had a passenger capacity of 1,200, only 64 were present on the maiden voyage; mechanical difficulties did not make them happy customers. Within a month the problems were rectified and the public gradually came to accept the new ship, and White Star, as a viable alternative to Cunard.

With the success of the *Oceanic*, Ismay and Imrie were not about to throw away the mold that created her. It was used to generate siblings that were similar, such as the *Atlantic, Baltic,* and *Republic,* and then enlarged to accommodate the *Adriatic* and *Celtic.* The company's early success, however, was punctuated by one massive failure: the loss of the *Atlantic.*

She was wrecked on the rocks off Nova Scotia in April 1873. There were 942 on board, of whom 481 perished, making it the nineteenth century's worst transatlantic disaster. Omniscient hindsight invites us to see this tragedy as a harbinger of what would happen during the same month thirty-nine years later. The parallels are uncanny. Like the *Titanic*, the *Atlantic's* misfortune occurred on a clear calm night. In both scenarios the presence of danger—rocks in 1873, ice in 1912—was well known. Other similarities include the captain not being at the helm and the ship traveling at almost full speed.

The incident became a media cause célèbre. Speculation was rife that the ship was low on coal and trying to take a dangerous shortcut. The captain behaved heroically by helping the survivors until he became exhausted and was pulled into a lifeboat. Such valor led to "only" a two year suspension, after which he was back at the helm for White Star.

One wonders how thoroughly the lesson of the *Atlantic* was imparted from Thomas Ismay to his son Bruce, who took over management of the line after the death of his father in 1899. Bruce Ismay went on to became the *Titanic's* most notorious survivor. Although he was, in his own words, "just a passenger," he nevertheless consulted regularly with the captain whenever navigational decisions were at issue.

A major factor in White Star's success was their liaison with the Harland and Wolff shipyards of Belfast. The Belfast shipbuilding industry had started in 1792 with the construction of the 300-ton *Hibernia*. In 1849 facilities were expanded to accommodate the construction of iron ships. In 1854 Edward James Harland arrived on the scene to became manager of a small local shipyard; it signaled a new beginning. Sailing ships, freighters, naval vessels, and tankers would continue to be built, but now the Belfast repertoire would include liners, which would bring more notoriety than all the other types of vessel combined. In 1858, Harland took complete control of the yard, along with his assistant Gustav Willhelm Wolff, who would become a full partner in 1861.

In 1863, William James Pirrie, a Canadian of Scottish-Irish parentage, joined Harland and Wolff as an apprentice draftsman at age fifteen. Pirrie became a full partner by 1874 and managing director in 1895 after the death of Harland. It was Pirrie who, in collaboration with Bruce Ismay and White Star, would plan the Olympic class liners. Illness prevented him from making the *Titanic* voyage, which was all to the good: he would have either perished or been vilified for having survived a disaster that partly resulted from shortcomings in the design of his ship. Pirrie weathered the aftermath of the tragedy and continued to build ships. He became Lord Pirrie in 1909 and died of pneumonia in 1924, appropriately enough at sea.

When Harland and Wolff built the *Oceanic* for White Star in 1871, it marked the beginning of a long and mutually beneficial collaboration. Harland and Wolff were the shipping line's sole builder throughout White Star's history until the merger with Cunard in 1934. The marriage was not without an ulterior logic. Gustav Wolff was the nephew of Gustavus Schwabe, who had provided the primary capital for Thomas Ismay to purchase and revamp White Star. The fortunes of the two companies were also drawn together by the trust White Star had in Harland and Wolff's contractual policy. Instead of charging a fixed price for the building of a ship—which, given vicissitudes in the cost of materials and labor, could entail a risk on their part—the arrangement was "cost plus." In other words, the shipping company paid for the building of the vessel, ceding complete jurisdiction in this area to Harland and Wolff, and then added a 4 percent commission to the total.

The quality of the Harland and Wolff ships helped make White Star competive with Cunard throughout the 1880s and 1890s. Cunarders, normally built in Glasgow, were slightly faster; White Star vessels were more elaborate. Glasgow had less costly access than Belfast to coal, timber, and steel, which by this time had displaced iron as the primary medium for ship construction, being stronger and 15 percent lighter. Belfast had lower rents and labor costs. It was a balanced competition and a near monopoly for the two giants until, in 1889, Germany decided to enter the sweepstakes as a major player.

On a visit to England that year, Kaiser Wilhelm II, grandson of Queen Victoria, was so impressed by the White Star's *Teutonic*—certainly the name must have appealed to him—that he decided to commit substantial resources to bolstering his nation's mercantile fleet. Previously, many German vessels had been built at British shipyards, including Harland and Wolff. During the 1890s, the Germans instead imported British engineers and craftsmen. They were lured by high salaries and became instrumental in establishing a major shipbuilding industry in Germany. The results of this enterprise were not long in coming.

In 1897 North German Lloyd launched the 650 foot *Kaiser Wilhelm de Grosse*. Capable of carrying 2,300 passengers at 21 knots, she soon snatched from Cunard the coveted Blue Riband for the fastest Atlantic crossing. British observers were further shocked in 1900 when she became the first transatlantic liner to be equipped with wireless, especially since early breakthroughs applying this medium to maritime communication had been done by Marconi working in England.

Before Cunard had a chance to recapture the Blue Riband, another German vessel, HAPAGs *Deutschland*, laid claim to it in 1900. Back it went to North German Lloyd in 1903, via the *Kaiser Wilhelm II*. Cunard bided their time until 1907 and then responded with the *Mauretania* and *Lusitania*. The *Mauretania* streaked across in 4 days, 10 hours, and 41 minutes, and enabled Cunard to rule the realm of speed for the next 22 years.

In 1929, North German Lloyd, having made a remarkable recovery from the devastation of World War I, recaptured the prize with the *Bremen*. The *Mauretania*, like an aging fighter with a few good moves still left, tried for the title one last time. She gave it her all, bettered her previous best, but still came up four hours short. This glorious competition of the great liners ultimately resulted in the current record, set in 1952 by the SS *United States*, of 3 days, 10 hours, and 40 minutes, which was done at an average speed of about 35 knots. Her true top speed, a closely guarded secret during her years of service, was close to 40 knots.

Although speed obsessed, the German ship industry at the turn of the century also wanted to make its vessels luxurious. North German Lloyd and Cunard were competitors with respect to record setting, so were HAPAG and White Star in the domain of elegant appointments. HAPAG's director, Albert Ballin, commissioned architect Charles Mewès to design interiors for the *Amerika,* slated to go into service in 1903. Mewès brought to this project his extensive experience working for hotel magnate, César Ritz. He came up with a decor that was both refined and understated; it included a stylish à-la-carte restaurant operated by Ritz personnel, which garnered rave reviews.

Despite the high profile the transatlantic passenger ship industry enjoyed at this time, it was becoming increasingly vulnerable economically. The competition among the various companies, which a decade earlier had seemed to benefit all players, now threatened any operation showing signs of weakness. The government-assisted German industry had Cunard and White Star looking over their shoulders whenever they were not looking sideways at each other. The race would still have its winner, or even winners, but also-rans could accrue major financial losses and end up insolvent.

These rivalries kept passenger fares low and threatened profit margins. In addition, the emigrant trade, which had partly inspired the large ships, was in a slack period. The lavish vessels had to be filled with all classes of passengers for the industry to remain healthy. They also had to be increasingly lavish to continue attracting the elite clientele we so often think of when we conjure up images of "La Belle Epoque." But as historian Barbara Tuchman has insistently noted, it was not "belle" for everyone. The unfettered accumulation of fabulous entrepreneurial fortunes was accompanied by considerable poverty, low-paying jobs, and economic fluctuations leading to high unemployment.

One way of stabilizing the situation, tempering the intense competition, and further developing the industry's public profile was regulation. Not regulation along government lines—the period was, after all, still dominated by the theory and practice of classical capitalism—but by drawing as many rivals as possible into a conglomerate. It was an intricate and potentially risk-laden project, but one that inspired American financier John Pierpoint Morgan. In 1902 he expanded one of his more modest holdings, the International Navigation Company of Philadelphia, into International Mercantile Marine, a trust devoted to acquiring as many shipping lines as possible. Morgan played monopoly in a way that made the concept represented in the later board game seem tame—indeed, the game itself was inspired by his machinations and it is Morgan's likeness we see in the logo of the mustachioed character wearing a top hat and holding the bag of money.

Those in control of the British government and economy, always resentful of any incursion into their realm of maritime dominance, found Morgan an anathema for two reasons. First, he was symptomatic of the transference of industrial wealth from Europe to the United States that had started following the Civil War; by the turn of the century, the United States was emerging as the world's leading industrial power.

Second, as an individual, Morgan was disdained for his acquisitive megalomania. In the dominant ideology of late Victorian and Edwardian Britain, power and privilege were supposed to be not only hereditary *but also responsible.* This is not to suggest that self-made wealth and nonaristocratic entrepreneurs were uncommon; they existed in the very industry under discussion. But what was rare, at least prior to Thatcherism, was the notion that one individual, a Morgan for example, could or should control a vast financial empire composed of diverse and even unrelated companies. Many Americans at the time labeled him an audacious predator. The British were hard pressed to find a relevant category in their vocabulary. Nevertheless, a major portion of their shipping business would become willing prey.

Morgan was on a roll when he formed International Mercantile Marine (IMM). A year earlier he had celebrated the turn of the century by buying out Andrew Carnegie to form the world's first billion dollar holding company, U.S. Steel. Steel was of course crucial to the railroad industry, which comprised another Morgan empire; to have easy access to it made entry into the realm of shipping that much more viable.

In quick succession IMM grabbed the Red Star, Leyland, and Dominion Lines, then Morgan cast for bigger fish—White Star and Cunard. The former proved to be the more vulnerable, largely because of the intercession of William Pirrie of Harland and Wolff. Pirrie was a member of the British board of IMM and had previously assisted Morgan in several acquisitions. The arrangement assured further contracts for Pirrie's firm. White Star was his biggest customer, and its future seemed more secure inside than outside the combine. Using this argument, he persuaded a reluctant Bruce Ismay to sell. Ismay retained his chairmanship and within a year was persuaded by Morgan to assume the presidency of IMM. He accepted with reservations, perhaps feeling the taint of tokenism. Nevertheless, his background and organizational skill helped save the trust from collapse when bouts of panic selling by stockholders plagued its early years. Not until 1927 would White Star be returned to Britsh ownership.

To the negotiations between IMM and the British companies, Morgan added a magnanimous but calculated gesture. Even though American owned, their ships could be coopted by the British Navy in case of war. From our vantage point in history this can seem an unenviable commitment in the event, say, of a possible war between Britain and a continental rival, Germany for instance, in which the United States might wish to remain neutral. But it may have been a peace offering aimed at mending fences between Britain and the United States, which had been noticeably disturbed several years earlier when, in 1895, the Americans claimed that Britain, in her Guyana colony, was overextending the frontier into Venezuela and therefore violating the Monroe Doctrine.

It has been said of Genghis Khan that the extent of his conquests were due partly to not knowing when to stop. Morgan is an equally apt candidate for this observation. With White Star in one hand and reaching for Cunard with the other, he eyed the German shipping industry. Securing Albert Ballin's help, IMM acquired 51 percent of HAPAG and then worked out a similar arrangement with North German Lloyd. The terms allowed the German companies to maintain considerable autonomy—more than was ceded to White Star—and their traditional domestic and foreign rivalries. The Kaiser saw—or at least rationalized—the deal as a way of insuring that British shipping would never dominate German.

The one prize that eluded Morgan was Cunard. He made generous overtures. He then tried force, by cutting fares on the IMM routes over which he had effective control. Cunard held fast and continued the daunting task of flying the flag of British shipping in the face of American corporate expansion. The head of the line, Lord Inverclyde, handled the situation deftly. He used each upping of the ante by Morgan as leverage to convince the government to step in. The government argued instead for the formation of a British combine to counter the American, but Inverclyde knew this would result in Cunard losing significant autonomy. The press was in his corner; Morganaphobia had fuelled national pride and Cunard was seen as a sterling example of Britian's maritime accomplishment. A loan from the British government to bolster Cunard's fleet and make it competitive with IMM was finally secured: 2.6 million pounds at 2¾ percent. There was one chauvinistic string attached: no foreigners could serve as directors, masters, officers, or engineers on Cunard ships.

The money was well spent, helping to bring into service in 1907 the *Lusitania* and *Mauretania*. The new Cunarders were not only the fastest liners yet built but were also the largest, exceeding White Star's biggest vessels in gross tonnage by 50 percent. Their arrival sent shock waves throughout International Mercantile Marine. For Pirrie and Ismay it meant back to the drawing board, or to be more precise, the drawing room.

On a pleasant summer evening in 1907—the exact date seems to have gone unrecorded—the two men and their wives enjoyed a soirée at Pirrie's elegant Belgravia home. The occasion produced pleasant conversation, dinner, and finally serious conversation and a plan. Cunard's lead could not go unchallenged. To try building anything faster than her two superliners would be folly on two counts. First, the fuel costs necessary to operate such a vessel would be exhorbitant. Each knot of extra speed over about twenty-one knots requires a disproportionate increase in the amount of coal consumed; at twenty-five knots the Cunarders were, in contemporary parlance, gas guzzlers. The second reason to forego a sprinter's mentality was that such ships were prone to annoying vibration, which a few knots less speed greatly reduced.

By evening's end a scheme emerged that favored the building of three liners designed to be larger and more comfortable than the Cunarders. The decision was an extension of the legacy that Thomas Ismay and William Imrie had started in 1871. The increase in the size of the liners, although substantial, was of the same magnitude by which their previous liners had just been surpassed by Cunard. But, at 45,000 tons and a length of almost 900 feet, they would be pushing what was at the time regarded as the theoretical size limit for conventional liners. Docks, especially in New York, would have to be modified to accommodate them, but more immediately, so would construction facilities at Harland and Wolff.

The plan was bold, but all parties involved had the kind of experience that evokes confidence. It certainly inspired J.P. Morgan. Grandiosity was his forte, and, perhaps still miffed by his failure to acquire Cunard, he sized on this opportunity to exert competitive superiority by quickly approving the proposal.

In December 1908 construction began on the *Olympic,* and in March 1909, in the adjoining slip, the *Titanic* followed suit. The third member of this triumverate was to have been called the *Gigantic,* but after the loss of the *Titanic,* the name was changed to the *Britannic.* White Star later denied they had ever conceived the original name, but a promotional flyer shows otherwise. Like the *Titanic,* the *Britannic* had a very short life. She went into service during the war in 1915, and while on duty as a hospital ship less than a year later, either hit a mine or was torpedoed. Despite sinking in less than an hour with 1,100 on board, only 30 lives were lost.

Progress in the construction of the *Olympic* and *Titanic,* and speculation about how closely the reality would match the promise, was avidly discussed in trade and technical journals and occasionally in the press. On 20 October 1910, without fanfare or a formal christening (White Star's disinterest in this ritual would give the superstitious something to ponder after the sinking of the *Titanic*), the *Olympic* was launched and towed to another venue to be fitted for service. Then, on 31 May 1911, with a little more pomp, which included the presence of Morgan and numerous other VIPs, the *Titanic* slipped majestically into the harbor. That day also saw the

Olympic handed over to White Star; with Ismay, Morgan, et al., on board, she steamed to Liverpool.

Both the *Olympic* and the *Titanic* offered enormous interior space within an overall design that suffered only slightly in comparison with their smaller faster rivals. Almost forgotten today by the public at large, the *Olympic* was a vessel that served long and dutifully. She did almost everything her wayward sister was reputed to be capable of doing, and has become the darling of maritime historians—perhaps the leading candidate for greatest liner ever. Her passenger capacity was 2,400, and on the maiden voyage she took a respectable 50 percent of that number to New York. The highly touted facilities functioned well. Passengers dined heartily; they could then burn off the calories in a gym endowed with the latest high tech apparatus, go for a swim in the pool, or have a Turkish bath. The less energetic could take an elevator to the spectator's gallery of the squash courts and watch others work up a sweat.

During World War I, the *Olympic* made a successful transition from luxury liner to troop carrier. In this service she survived several submarine attacks. In one instance she turned and rammed the offending U-boat, which promptly sank. This bit of derring-do earned her the sobriquet, "Old Reliable." In 1919 she became the first large liner converted from coal to diesel. In 1934 she was involved in another collision, this one less heroic. She accidently rammed and sank the Nantucket lightship, resulting in the loss of all seven crew members and a lawsuit against White Star. Add to this the *Hawke* incident of 1911, and her collision total stands at three. Her final violent confrontation would be at the hands of the wrecker in 1935. With the *Queen Mary* on the way, the newly merged Cunard White Star Line decided to cull its fleet. Ironically, the *Olympic*'s great rival, the *Mauretania*, was also on this death list. As befitted her legendary speed, she went to the block first.

The *Titanic* was designed as an ultradeluxe version of the *Olympic*. She started with the same basic plan: spacious dining areas and lounges, pool, gymnasium, and labyrinthian interior that caused even crew members to lose their way on occasion. Ismay's experience on the *Olympic*, however, led him to conjure several modifications: passenger capacity was increased to slightly over 3,000 by converting excess deck space into cabins; exquisite carpets and hardwood furniture were added to the Grand Saloon and several smaller venues; glass paneling was installed on the first-class promenade deck; and two opulent first-class suites were constructed, one for J. P. Morgan (who, although present at the launch, was prevented by illness from making the maiden voyage). The list was augmented with dozens of other changes, the two most notable (in light of postdiscovery interest in the ship) being the lavish grand staircase of polished oak, illuminated by a glass dome framed in wrought iron, and the Café Parisien and adjoining boulevard.

At 46,000 tons, the *Titanic*'s extra frills made her 1,000 tons heavier than her elder sister. In terms of power, the two ships were virtually identical, transferring 50,000 horsepower to a conventional two-screw setup, with a third turbine-driven shaft in the center. They also shared the same inadequate complement of twenty lifeboats, which only had between 1,100 and 1,200 places. This was not an oversight. It complied with, even exceeded, the arcane British Board of Trade regulations that based the number of lifeboats a ship carried solely on her tonnage. Discussion had been given to increasing the number of boats, but Ismay vetoed the idea in order to permit more recreational space on the decks in question. The general feeling on the part of those concerned with the building of the ship was that she was as close to unsinkable as any vessel could be—a virtual giant lifeboat. This sentiment, when transmogrified into folkloric legend, became "the ship that God himself cannot sink."

The question of the ship's unsinkability, a minor issue prior to the voyage, has now become an essential theme in most discussions of the disaster. White Star has always denied making the claim, attributing it to the media. New evidence has recently emerged to refute their disavowal. A White Star flyer promoting the *Olympic* and *Titanic*, brought to light in the February–April 1993 issue of the *Titanic Commutator* by Geoff Robinson and Don Lynch, ends by noting that "as far as it is possible to do so, these two wonderful vessels are designed to be unsinkable." Ismay himself had the courage to admit to the British Board of Trade Inquiry that prior to the sinking he did believe the ship to be "practically unsinkable . . . a lifeboat unto herself."

This confidence was no doubt a result of the ship's design. She was divided into sixteen watertight compartments that could be sealed with electrically operated sliding doors. The problem was that these compartments were, in effect, only semiwatertight. Although extending above the waterline, the transverse bulkheads did not reach to the top deck. When more than two became flooded at the bow after the collision, the weight pulled the ship down headfirst, causing water to spill over into the next compartment, and the next, and so on.

Postsinking hindsight has led to speculation that, given the ship's design, a better course of action might have been to ram the iceberg head-on instead of reversing engines and turning the helm. The *Arizona* in 1879, and several other vessels in the decades prior to the sinking of the *Titanic*, had survived encounters with ice by doing this, although it was not a conscious strategy. Another theory argues that it was a mistake to reverse engines when turning the helm, since the result was to impede the ship's capacity to maneuver effectively. The most recent example of omniscient hindsight claims it was a mistake to close the electrically operated collision doors on the watertight bulkheads. This allowed water to accumulate too rapidly in the bow, thereby exacerbating flooding in the rest of the ship when the bow started to go under. By letting the ship flood evenly it might have been possible to gain another hour or two.

All this second-guessing converges on First Officer Murdoch, who was in charge of the bridge that night and for whom we should have considerable sympathy. If only he had been given world enough and time. The agonizingly brief interval—probably less than a minute—between when lookout Frederick Fleet sighted the iceberg, relayed the information to Murdoch, and the collision occurred, will no doubt continue to provide an eternity for speculation.

Part II

WIRELESS WORLD

It seemed as if the stars above saw the ship in distress and had awakened to flash messages across the black dome of the sky to each other.

—Lawrence Beesley, *Titanic* survivor

On a brisk January morning in 1986, the *Challenger* lifted skyward from Cape Canaveral while millions watched on live television. Within moments, curiosity and anxiety turned to confusion and shocked fascination. The ambitiously conceived space-bound vehicle exploded like a Roman candle. It filled our screens with an image that might have been dazzling and exquisite were it not for the horrifying implications. The *Challenger* was designed as a technological womb for a handful of intrepid explorers whom the media had presented as intriguing personalities. It became a blazing tomb that interred itself in the North Atlantic, 2,000 miles from where the *Titanic* had come to rest 74 years earlier.

Watching the *Challenger* self-destruct on live television imparted an involvement in the event to a mass audience. This kind of experience is sometimes referred to as "co-presence" or "simultaniety"—things distant in space are perceived at the same moment in time, regardless of the location of the observer. News stories that employ this technique can be particularly riveting. Early examples familiar to North Americans date from the Golden Age of Radio during the 1930s. They include the crash of the *Hindenberg* (1937)—although a delayed broadcast, it nevertheless gave listeners a sense of being there—and Orson Welles's dramatization of the *War of the Worlds* (1938). Earlier, in Britain, the Crystal Palace fire in London (1936) was snared by this new journalism: a young reporter named Richard Dimbleby managed to secure a telephone within earshot of the action and, with the chaotic soundscape of the fire in the background, described the situation live over BBC radio.

The reportage of all these events was anticipated, although on a smaller scale, by the circumstances that surrounded the *Titanic* during the early morning hours of 15 April 1912. As would be the case with the *Challenger*, individuals thousands of miles away knew something was amiss even before the drama played to its conclusion. Wireless communication made this possible.

Like the telegraph and telephone, wireless was a medium for rapid point-to-point communication. Morse code rather than voice was the dominant form for messages prior to the 1920s. Wireless transmission did not constitute broadcasting, as we now understand the term, but it was far less discrete than using the telegraph or telephone. A message radiated in all directions, hence the synonym "radiotelegraphy," then simply "radio" after 1912. Anyone with an adequate receiver could listen in.

With the *Titanic*'s distress call, and its subsequent ship-to-shore relays, the listening network included marine, commercial, and military operators, as well as a growing legion of amateurs. It was the largest "audience" ever to receive a series of related transmissions. As a result, wireless communication attained a visibility and significance that had only been hinted at on the several previous occasions where its use for rescue at sea had made headlines. Never before had so many lives been at stake; never before had the medium performed so nobly; and never before had it fallen so short of its true potential. In the aftermath of the disaster, changes in wireless policy were demanded by the press and at both formal inquiries.

And, just as wireless became a major player in the *Titanic*'s bizarre theater of tragedy, so this tragedy became a pivotal moment in the history of the new medium. In the midst of it all the name Guglielmo Marconi (1874–1937) achieved the proverbial household status, both for his invention of wireless and his involvement in the events of April 1912.

3

Marconi and
Maritime Communication

On 10 April 1912, Marconi's wife Beatrice and their three-year-old daughter Degna longingly watched the *Titanic* steam past their country cottage near Southampton. The entire family had been invited by the White Star Line to be special guests on this maiden voyage. Circumstances intervened. Marconi had left three days earlier on the *Lusitania*. He was in a hurry to get to New York and had a pile of business correspondence to attend to—the *Lusitania* had an excellent stenographer and this figured in his decision. Beatrice and family were expected to follow on the *Titanic*, but when baby Giulio came down with a fever, they were forced to delay their travel plans. Marconi's return to England was also supposed to have been aboard the *Titanic*. The tragedy intervened, rearranging his schedule and the fortunes of his company.

Thus unfolds the central chapter of a story whose opening scene begins in 1894 in Beillese, Italy, with the youthful Marconi engaged in a series of electrical experiments. His goal: to send Morse code without the use of wires. The advantages of this kind of telegraphy? It would be a means of communication whereby messages could travel at the speed of light to and from places where it is not feasible to run wires, such as ship-to-ship and ship-to-shore. A warm supportive mother, Scottish-Irish Annie Jameson, overrode the influence of a dour skeptical father. She took the precocious Marconi to England, where more interest and funding could be directed toward his work.

In 1896 Marconi filed a patent for his wireless. Throughout his life he would continue to upgrade the invention, but his attention now turned to its practical application and commercial potential. He envisioned a global communications empire based on his invention. This dream would be most fully realized following the sinking of the *Titanic*. It would also be vulnerable at this time to regulatory decisions aimed at limiting the controls that a company could have over such a strategic technological resource.

In July 1897, Marconi and a small coterie of supporters set up the Wireless Telegraph and Signal Company, Ltd. Up to that point, Marconi had been working under the auspices of the British Postal Service, which had offered continued support, but the entrepreneurial freedom of going the private commercial route seemed worth the risks. The immediate goals of the new company were twofold: to set up a viable network of marine communications and then, after further development of the apparatus, to establish transatlantic communication of sufficient reliability that regular service would follow. Today, when we think of using the airwaves for communication, more precisely the electromagnetic spectrum, we usually think of broadcasting—the aural and video dissemination of information and entertainment to a mass audience. It is sometimes difficult to imagine that the early history of this form of telecommunications was tied to point-to-point exchanges between ships and shore stations using Morse code. A brief look at the world of transportation and communication around the turn of the century reveals why this was so.

The transoceanic ship industry was big business. It moved an ever increasing volume of goods and people around the world. North Atlantic routes between Europe and America were particularly busy. The immigrant trade was a lucrative aspect of this enterprise, and even the *Titanic*, despite her splendor and the rich and famous passengers she attracted, was expected to earn most of her income this way.

By 1900 ships were relatively fast. A top liner could span the Atlantic in under six days, or about the same amount of time it took to cross the North American continent by train. The major problem with these ocean voyages was the complete isolation that enveloped the ship when she was out of sight of land and other ships. Visual communication was limited to about one hundred yards using semaphore flags, and a few miles at best when employing Morse lamp at night; sometimes carrier pigeons were used, but the practice was never widespread.

Compare this situation with overland travel by road or rail, where the telegraph and telephone provided an accompanying information network and lifeline. When a train was late, the reasons could be signaled down the line, often in a matter of minutes. When an ocean liner was late, patience was strained and anxiety resulted. She could be off course, perhaps experiencing bad weather. Mechanical difficulties might be the culprit. Or it could be more serious. The ship might be foundering as a result of a collision or fire. But where? Marconi's wireless promised deliverance from this centuries-old dilemma. Ships could now be monitored like trains, not only for safety and navigation, but also to prepare ports for their arrival and to relay relevant news.

Before Marconi could sell his service to commercial and government interests, however, he had to sell them first on the idea and its feasibility. This required considerable acumen. Not all great inventors have been adept in dealing with those they wish to convince, but Marconi had the "right stuff" when it came to this kind of interpersonal communication. He spoke fluent English and was neither the wild-eyed unkempt stereotype of an inventor nor its antithesis, a dull abstract theorist. His public persona, especially when dealing with the press, was that of a humble and creative young man who, although exceedingly well dressed, was always modest and cordial—the embodiment of understated brilliance. The many positive depictions of him in newspapers and magazines converged in the aftermath of the *Titanic* disaster. As a result, his image easily weathered the potentially scandalous and well-founded accusation that his corporate machinations with the *New York Times*—to guarantee the paper an exclusive interview with the *Titanic*'s surviving wireless operator—were not in the public interest.

Behind the scenes, Marconi was somewhat more aloof and obsessive. He was both the wizard and warlord of wireless. A wizard: not in the sense of pure inventive genius, but because of his ability to improve and make practical the work of numerous predecessors. The warlord: it derived from an ambition to see the Marconi version of wireless become the world's standard and from the accompanying strategies he developed to protect his lead and keep at bay competing organizations with a similar agenda. Consistent with Marconi's more tempered public image was his opposition, in 1900, to his company's name change. His sole dissenting vote was overridden and the Wireless Telegraph and Signal Company became the Marconi Wireless Telegraph Company, Ltd.

Marconi's campaign to make wireless an indispensable aspect of maritime endeavor began in earnest in 1898. The Italian Navy adopted his system, thus rewarding a native son whose early and successful experiments were done in Italy, although they had been denied funding by her government. More relevant to potential British investors, however, was Marconi's coverage that year of the Kingston Regatta for the Dublin *Daily Express*. He followed the races in a motor launch and transmitted late-breaking developments. The press was impressed. That summer he was given the opportunity to install his system on the Royal Yacht *Osborne*, where the Prince of Wales (later Edward VII), was recuperating from a twisted knee. The shore unit was set up at Ladywood Cottage on the grounds of Osborne House. The yacht was two miles out and blocked from view by intervening hills. The experiment succeeded and Queen Victoria was able to monitor the progress of her son's recovery. On 4 August the *Osborne* sent the first medical bulletin in wireless history.

Events moved with increased rapidity in 1899. In January, after a month-long trial, regular wireless service was adopted by the East Goodwin light-house and lightship. When the *Elbe* ran aground in March the new medium saved lives and cargo. The admiralty expressed interest and began testing the system for possible adoption by the British Navy. By this time, both sides of the Atlantic were aware of Marconi's efforts, a situation facilitated by his deft rapport with the press. Several Americans, among them the editors of the *New York Herald* and *Evening Telegram*, began to suspect that Marconi and his wireless might someday enter the hallowed pantheon of inventive renown that included the likes of Morse, Bell, and Edison. They made him an offer he could not refuse: $5,000 to cover the America's Cup sailing races for them in October. What ultimately made Marconi acquiesce was not the money but the potential publicity.

The significance of the America's Cup as a field-test, or perhaps we should say sea-test, of wireless cannot be underestimated. The event, pitting the American ship, *Columbia* (the eventual winner), against the British represen-tative, *Shamrock*, was both a sporting and cultural celebration. It made head-lines for half the month, not only in the *Herald* and *Telegram* but also in the *New York Times*. Other notable stories, such as the Boer War and Dewey's visit to New York, were often consigned to secondary status.

The logistics of coverage entailed that three ships be equipped with wire-less. At first the *Ponce*, and later the *Grande Duchesse*, followed the races and relayed coverage to the *MacKay Bennett*, which was anchored offshore and linked by cable to the news networks of the "wired world." Marconi's enter-prise was noticed. Wireless worked. After the races he transferred to the Navy the sets that were used for further testing and possible adoption, then pro-ceeded to set up the Marconi Wireless Telegraph Company of America—in this context, unlike in the British, he did not question the wisdom of trading on his name.

In 1900, the Marconi parent company spawned another subsidiary, the Marconi International Marine Communications Company, and signed its first commercial contract to put wireless aboard the German steamship *Kaiser Wilhelm de Grosse* and, with the permission of the German government, to also equip a lighthouse and lightship. Germany at this time was Britain's chief rival for seagoing supremacy. She also had a fledgling wireless company, Tele-funken, which used the Marconi-inspired Slaby-Arco system. The decision to go with the Marconi company in this instance was based on commercial rather than national considerations. On the one hand, Marconi Marine had an already established network of shore stations; on the other, it limited the effectiveness of its smaller rivals by invoking the controversial "nointercommunications" policy.

"Nointercommunications" meant that Marconi Marine forbade its operators to relay or respond to the messages of other companies, save in an emergency. This facilitated the corporate quest for monopoly. The public rationale was that rival companies, such as Telefunken, should not be allowed to make use of the Marconi network of shore stations since they did not contribute to their maintenance. In 1902, this policy created an international incident when Prince Henry, brother of the Kaiser, while returning to Germany from the United States aboard the *Deutschland*, a Telefunken ship, could not get his diplomatic communiqués forwarded. According to historian Susan Douglas, this incident was a major factor in the convening of the first international conference on wireless a year later.

By 1900, the Royal Navy and Cunard had subscribed to the Marconi service. In 1901 Lloyd's of London came on board. Pun intended, marine insurance was a major aspect of their business. Lloyd's advocated that ships holding policies with them adopt the Marconi wireless, which would link them to the worldwide network of Lloyd's offices being conjoined this way.

Not only did large companies, like the White Star Line, subscribe to the service but also those of more modest means, who felt it was a worthwhile and affordable option. The reason is one familiar to many of us: purchase of the apparatus was not necessary. Marconi leased his equipment, along with a trained operator, and did not charge for individual messages. To further insure control, he refused to sell his equipment. Exceptions were made in the case of the Italian and British navies, but they had to pay an annual royalty after the initial purchase. Marconi made a similar offer to the United States Navy. They were suspicious, and the negotiations did not go as smoothly as with his other contracts. In 1903, after the failed talks with Marconi and several tests of competitor's equipment, the United States Navy went wireless by purchasing the Slaby-Arco system and training their own operators.

The successful expansion of marine wireless began to demonstrate conclusively what Marconi had insisted when he first went into business: wireless signals were not limited to line-of-sight transmission. He believed they followed the curvature of the earth and had a range that was potentially limitless, given the use of low-frequency long waves and a high-power transmitter. Why this is so was not clear, nor did the gap in electromagnetic theory perturb him. What counted was what worked, rather than high level explanations of why. In 1899 he spanned the English Channel, and soon after ships were picking up transmissions hundreds of miles distant. Concessions from the naysayers, which included some of the most eminent scientists in the field, gradually came.

Further evidence for the long-range capacity of wireless came in December 1901. A successful transatlantic signal made it from Poldhu, in the west of England, to the receiving station manned by Marconi on Signal Hill near St. John's, Newfoundland. It was a simple message, a static-filled letter S: three dots in Morse code. When the event was reported almost everyone rejoiced, except the cable companies, who claimed infringement on their international telegraph monopoly when cable stocks dropped as a result. The press, as usual, was on Marconi's side. So was Alexander Graham Bell, who invited Marconi to set up shop on his property in Cape Breton, Nova Scotia, which, unlike Newfoundland, had no cable company contract. One year later a full message was sent, followed in January 1903 by greetings from President Theodore Roosevelt to King Edward VII.

Not only Bell but Thomas Edison as well expressed admiration for this aspirant to their ranks. In the au courant journal, the *World's Works*, Edison remarked: "Give Marconi ten years and he will be sending 1,000 words a minute by wireless." It never happened, but in 1907 regular transatlantic service did. At 5¢ per word for the press and 10¢ for others, Marconi undercut the monopoly of the cable companies. They had been charging 25¢ per word and now had to reduce their rate to be competitive. That same year, the *New York Times* became an enthusiastic subscriber to the new service, beginning a relationship that would play a strategic role in its coverage of the *Titanic* disaster. In October a new supplement was introduced to the Sunday *Times*, the "Marconi Transatlantic Wireless Dispatches."

The more that marine wireless was used in the early years of the new century, the more various uses for it were envisioned. Navigation and shipping dispatches began to be interspersed with late-breaking news, European or North American, depending on the ship's proximity to either continent. Should the vessel be beyond the range of shore stations, important information could be relayed, ship to ship, to almost any point in the North Atlantic.

The newsletters on larger liners began to include current world news in their pages, a trend started by the *Cunard Daily Bulletin*, with its supplement, "Marconigrams—direct to the ship." It was claimed, and with some validity, that passengers halfway across the Atlantic were often more in touch with world events than many people on land. And when the wireless was not engaged in any of these functions, it could be used to send personal telegrams, a service that, given the *Titanic's* illustrious and wealthy passengers, kept both her operators regularly engaged. With such maximal use of the medium almost from its outset, some kind of international consensus had to be reached regarding wireless regulation.

The first International Wireless Telegraphy Conference was held in Madrid in 1903. Although the meeting was convened primarily to sort out issues rather than to mandate specific policy, it did ask participating nations to recommend to their governments that it should be obligatory for all coastal stations to receive and transmit messages from all ships, regardless of their wireless company affiliation.

This challenge to the Marconi nointercommunications rule was restated at the 1906 International Conference on Wireless Communication at Sea held in Berlin. Britain acquiesced to the policy by a one vote majority in the House of Commons the following year (Marconi was opposed and he had many supporters in the House), and in 1908 it became law. Was it obeyed? Rarely. Except for emergency messages, non-Marconi transmissions were snubbed. Telefunken was frustrated, since many of their ships used the English Channel. To make matters worse for Germany, two of their shipping lines, HAPAG, and Bremer Lloyd, were Marconi subscribers; they could not, therefore, access most German shore stations and other German ships. Reconciliation came later that year when a new German company was formed. It was controlled by Telefunken, who had a 55 percent majority, with Marconi holding significant minority interests. The two giants could now intercommunicate.

Marconi's chief American competitor at this time, United Wireless, was still subject to the now "unofficial" nointercommunications rule. The rivalry between them eventually went to the courts, but over another issue: patent infringement by United. Marconi won most of the decisions and United went bankrupt. In fact, Marconi was in New York in April 1912 to consummate a takeover of what remained of United when the *Titanic* went down. With his stock soaring after the disaster, Marconi absorbed United's seventy shore stations and five hundred ship installations. This gave him a dominant presence not only on the eastern seaboard but in the Great Lakes as well.

Besides dealing with the nointercommunications issue, the 1906 Berlin conference proposed other legislation, which in turn was ratified by participating nations within two years. All ship stations and operators had to be licensed by their home countries. The minimum performance standard at the key was twelve words per minute—by this time auditory reception was the norm, having displaced the use of the printout paper strip that characterized both the Marconi and Slaby-Arco systems during their first years. Each ship was to have a three-letter call signature for easy identification; in the case of the *Titanic* this was what would become the legendary MGY. Also under negotiation were the call letters for an international distress signal. The British preferred CQD ($-\cdot-\cdot$ / $--\cdot-$ / $-\cdot\cdot$), for "seek you," the general call, with the addition of D for "danger." This was a staple of their railway-influenced telegraph service. The Germans found this solution too complex and chauvinistic. They suggested SOE ($\cdot\cdot\cdot$ / $---$ / $\cdot$), but it was pointed out that the final E could be obliterated in strong interference. Eventually SOS ($\cdot\cdot\cdot$ / $---$ / $\cdot\cdot\cdot$) was adopted, not because, as many later believed, it refers to save our souls or save our ship, but due to its distinct nature and ability to cut through overlapping transmissions and interference. Marconi had selected the letter S for the same reasons during his successful transatlantic efforts of December 1901.

Not until 1912, would SOS be accepted in practice as *the* official distress call, largely because of the *Titanic* disaster. But in the years between 1908 and 1912, despite ratification of the Madrid Convention, CQD was the preferred option, especially among Marconi operators. In 1909 this call, coupled with the idea of a ship in distress being dependent on wireless for the survival of her passengers, made front-page news in the most publicized ocean liner accident of the pre-*Titanic* wireless era.

On the fog-enshrouded morning of 23 January, at 5:30 A.M. in the coastal waters off Nantucket, the White Star liner *Republic* was accidentally rammed by the *Florida* of the Lloyd Italiano Line. The *Republic* was outbound, taking 461 passengers on a Mediterranean cruise. The *Florida* was inbound, loaded with nearly 1,000 immigrants. The collision ripped through the side of the *Republic*, causing serious structural damage and impeding the function of her wireless. The *Florida* was less imperiled, but did not have wireless. She limped back to help the endangered vessel, which by this time had closed her collision bulkheads. As the doomed *Republic*'s passengers were transferred to the *Florida*, her wireless operator, Jack Binns, who would later manage to join them remained on board. He valiantly and successfully struggled to repair the apparatus and send out a distress call. Several ships responded, among them the White Star's *Baltic*. She took the passengers from both stricken vessels to New York.

It was a sensational news story, almost miraculous in tenor given the many lives saved that could just as easily have been lost; the final tally of fatalities: two on the *Republic* and three on the *Florida*. A similar collision several years later, involving the Canadian Pacific ship *Empress of Ireland* in the Gulf of St. Lawrence on 29 May 1914, would claim 1,012. She sank in approximately 15 minutes, thereby rendering the wireless assisted rescue "too little, too late."

The *Republic*'s misfortune produced two heroes: wireless, and the ship's Marconi man, Jack Binns. Both were championed by the *New York Times*, which took the lead in presenting the story in considerable and often repetitive detail. Their coverage is worth a brief assessment here, since it became an unsuspected dress rehearsal for the *Times's* performance in the epoch-making maritime drama that would follow in April of 1912.

On Sunday, 24 January, the *Times's* headline noted the plight of the *Republic*. The subheadline read: "A Whole Company of Mighty Ships Called by Wireless to Her Aid." The lead article explained the call letters CQ and CQD; no mention was made of the "official," but as yet unused signal, SOS. The general manager of American Marconi, John Bottomley was interviewed. He modestly noted how wireless had done its job, then went over the sequence of transmissions that had been received. His comments give the impression that wireless communication was considerably more efficient and well organized than was the case, either in 1909 or 1912.

The *Times* followed this with a bit of audacious self-promotion that would have been in exceedingly bad taste, or probably omitted altogether, had casualties been higher. Readers were reminded of the paper's coverage of the fire on board the Phoenix Line's steamship *St. Cuthbert*, which had occurred on 4 February 1908, 200 miles off the coast of Nova Scotia. This incident was also characterized by a wireless-assisted rescue at sea, whereby the White Star's *Cymric* saved thirty-eight of fifty crewmen caught in the blaze. Since the *Times* office had been in direct contact with the *Cymric* by wireless, they proudly noted how it was possible for them to have exclusive coverage at a time when not a word about the event appeared in other New York papers. These comments, and the accompanying story about the *Republic* and *Florida*, appeared in a Sunday edition of the paper. The third section contained the weekly feature, "Marconi Transatlantic Wireless Dispatches," which must have further drawn readers' attentions to the new medium and the *Times's* wisdom in using it.

The edition of 25 January noted how *Republic* had been in tow when she finally sank, with the captain and crew barely managing to escape. On 26 January coverage included a statement from Marconi. He was pleased with the performance of his wireless, hoped more ships would adopt it, and mentioned that future instruments would have increased range. Another article introduced Jack Binns as the courageous wireless operator who, with the failed engines having killed the generator, waded through the icy waters of the storage room to get batteries so he could restart the apparatus.

On 27 January, Binns's heroics became the headline. An article told of him holding the transmitter together with one hand and signaling with the other while battling frigid conditions. In another, he recounted his own version of the events in a modest "ah shucks it was nothing" manner, which endeared him to the public. By 29 January he was a national celebrity. The *Times* described how, while attending a musical review, he was forced on stage to make a speech and then was mobbed by chorus girls. The French government recommended to the American that he be given a special tribute.

Binns emerged as his era's version of the great American hero, the real-life version of a Horatio Alger story. Various commentators have likened him to Tom Swift, the heroic young inventor depicted in a series of popular novels at the time, and Charles Lindbergh, who would become a champion for the next generation. He also became known as "CQD Binns," and in this capacity he encouraged a legion of young, primarily white middle-class males, to take up wireless as a hobby.

These amateurs often made their own sets, many with the hope that they too might one day play a role in some dramatic event and thereby attain their own celebrity. It rarely happened, and perhaps out of frustration a number of them turned to less honorable pursuits: they began to interfere with or jam commercial shipping and naval transmissions. This often took the form of obscene messages and, on several unnerving occasions, false alarms about sinking ships, a practice that was suspected when early reports of the *Titanic*'s plight were relayed to shore. A contemporary parallel to this can perhaps be seen in the case of computer hackers, who have access to information technology that can access the data banks of large institutions. Their virus implants and other mischief recall the efforts of these unscrupulous amateurs during the early prebroadcasting days of radio.

After the *Republic* incident, Binns left the wireless business and parlayed his fame into a successful career as a writer on maritime topics. In April 1912, he was in London as the *Titanic* was being readied for her maiden voyage. He gave thought to returning on the celebrated liner; Captain Smith was an old acquaintance—Binns had served with him for two years aboard the *Adriatic* before his posting on the *Republic*. A new job assignment in New York intervened and decided Binns's fate. Anxious to get there, he left on the *Minnesota* several days before the *Titanic* departed Southampton.

4

Wireless at Work

The bizarre sequence of events that immortalized the *Titanic* gave wireless communication the greatest challenge of its brief history. At first it was believed the medium performed up to expectations. But, as the magnitude and contingencies of the disaster were revealed, so was the failure of wireless to perform the full miracle of coordinating an immediate and complete rescue. The lesson of the *Titanic* dramatized what the near tragedy of the *Republic* had suggested to a handful of critics: the procedures of wireless communication had to be more comprehensive, given the volume and complexity of the transportation it monitored.

To understand the changes in regulatory policy that resulted, we must first consider the circumstances, and some of the messages, of wireless during the disaster. Such an examination can also help us grasp one of the *Titanic's* great enigmas and a paramount factor in her enduring fascination: the relationship between what was and what might have been.

When the *Titanic* departed Southampton on 10 April, she was endowed with the latest in wireless technology and two young but proven operators. The *Titanic's* Marconi equipment had a daytime range of 250-400 miles and a nighttime limit that occasionally surpassed 2,000 miles. We sometimes notice this difference in electromagnetic capacity when we tune our car radios at night to find a station that is interesting and audible, and discover that it is not local but hundreds of miles distant. Our failure to pick up the same station in daylight is due to the interference of solar radiation, a phenomenon little understood in 1912. Marconi and his operators left explanation of the discrepancy to scientists and used a practical understanding of it to schedule their longer-distance exchanges at night.

Power for MGY, the call letters of the *Titanic*'s station, came from the ship's electrical system. A battery-operated backup system was located nearby, should the primary source fail. High above the top deck a large antenna ran three-quarters of the ship's length, suspended between two towering masts; the antenna can be seen in almost all reproductions of the ship.

In charge of MGY's wireless transmissions were Jack Phillips, the senior operator who turned 25 on 11 April, and Harold Bride, 22. Phillips had served Marconi Marine on the *Teutonic, Campania, Oceanic,* and *Lusitania*; Bride also saw duty on the *Lusitania* and on the *Haverford, Lanfranc,* and *Anselm*. The two men were not formally a part of the crew and wore the uniform of Marconi Marine. Their life on board was largely confined to the wireless cabin. It had a tripartite structure, with two sections for equipment and one for sleeping. Phillips and Bride did not dine or socialize with the ship's officers, several of whom were unknown to them, and Phillips occasionally expressed his preference for the more personal atmosphere of a smaller vessel. Nevertheless, the status of working on the *Titanic* was unmatched; though the salary was not. The low pay of 15-20 dollars a month was thought to be offset by the glamor of the calling. During the American inquiry, Senator Smith questioned this. Given the importance of wireless operators as a liaison between shipping companies and the outside world, he felt they should be paid a salary commensurate with their responsibilities

Phillips, Bride, and the other operators on the giant liners that carried two Marconi men worked staggered shifts so that one of them would be on duty at all times. Most of the vessels within several hours of MGY when she sent her distress call, including the smaller Leyland ship *Californian* and the Cunarder *Carpathia*, carried but one. Despite the division of labor between Phillips and Bride, they worked shifts that were often exhausting.

A typical mélange of MGY exchanges included information on the position of nearby ships, weather bulletins, time signals, congratulatory wishes for the maiden voyage, and comments about floating debris. (In this last category, at least half-a-dozen ice warnings were received prior to the fatal collision.) During selected hours of the day, the wireless was also used for personal telegrams, which occasionally included business transactions worth thousands of dollars. On the evening of 14 April a backlog of personal messages faced the two Marconi men.

Another important assignment for wireless operators was to monitor the news of the day at scheduled intervals. It was received from the Marconi station at Poldhu in the west of England when the ship was within range, and from Cape Cod when signals from North America were easier to capture. A ship caught somewhere between the range of these two stations could have the information relayed to her by intermediate vessels. On White Star liners, this news was incorporated into an attractive magazine, the *Atlantic Daily Bulletin*. Most of its twelve pages were prepared ashore, with updates added en route. The publication contained essays on literature, the arts, science, and business. Minus the news entries, it can be seen as a forerunner of the general-interest magazines put out today by large airlines.

Marconi operators were a dedicated breed and their labor a true vocation. An extraordinary amount of time was spent at the headphones, and not just in the handling of official dispatches. Operators would often scan the airwaves to monitor the plethora of transmissions always present, thereby exploring the limits of the new technology. Operators were so skilled that many could distinguish a station by the tone of its signal or a fellow operator by his style in sending the dots and dashes of Morse code.

Like today's computer aficionados, wireless operators used many contractions and abbreviations to economize communication. For example, CQ was the general call; QRA, what is the name of your station; QRA MGY, the name of my station is the *Titanic*; TU OM GN, thank you old man, good night (an irony given the youth of most of the operators); QRT, keep quiet I'm busy; and sometimes GTH OM QRT, get to hell old man, keep quiet I'm busy. The latter is but a mild example of the off-color language that was occasionally used. It could became downright obscene when the receiving station belonged to a different wireless company, at times escalating to the point of a willful jamming of the competitor's signal. This practice was less prevalent with Marconi Marine than among its smaller rivals.

Part of a wireless operator's responsibilities included the maintenance of his equipment. This turned out to be crucial in the case of the *Titanic*. According to Bride, in a postrescue exclusive to the *New York Times*, the transmitter began to act up late on Friday, 12 April. The problem was traced to leads running from the transformer to the transmitter. They had burned through, making contact with the iron bolts that supported the apparatus, thus depleting its power. In the twenty-four hours prior to the collision, Phillips and Bride (mostly Phillips) put in nearly seven hours of crucial repair work. Bride's account implied that had they failed to resolve this problem, transmission of the distress signal would have been impossible. When Bride relieved Phillips on that fateful night, it was 12 midnight (Bride had slept through the collision, which had occurred at 11:40 P.M.), rather than the regularly scheduled 2 A.M., because of the long hours Phillips had already spent fixing the short.

Bride later speculated that the reason he survived and Phillips did not—both were thrown into the water and found their way to lifeboats—was because Phillips was already exhausted when the crisis began. It might also have been more than a coincidence that Bride's account of the wireless repair operation recalled the one performed by Jack Binns on the *Republic* three years earlier.

One of the great controversies surrounding wireless and the *Titanic* concerns her reception of numerous ice warnings, which began coming in at the start of the voyage. Despite this, the ship was steaming at her fastest speed, 22½ knots (just over 24 miles per hour, or close to 40 kilometers per hour) on the evening of 14 April. As later testimony would show, this practice was not unusual given a clear sky and calm sea. Captain Edward Smith, or E.J., as he was affectionately known, when informed of the presence of ice in the vicinity, rather than curb the ship's speed asked about the visibility. He stated that if it was questionable in the slightest, the ship would have to slow down. Given the seemingly ideal conditions, speed was maintained.

What E.J., with all his experience, and apparently most of the ship's officers did not realize was that conditions were in a sense "too good to be *true*," in the sense of both accuracy and validity. Movement in an object helps in the perception of it against a neutral background. Had there been waves from even a slight swell breaking against the base of the iceberg—which allegedly had its darker, or black-ice, side facing the ship—they might have reflected the available light and allowed the lookout, Fred Fleet, to see the iceberg several seconds sooner. At the later inquiries, several crewmen stated how the conditions of sea and air on that night were calmer than any they had ever experienced. Despite these conditions, and the posted ice warnings, none of the officers suggested to the captain that the ship's speed be curtailed.

Some of the ships involved in sending dispatches about ice were the *Caronia, Amerika, Baltic, Noordam, La Touraine, Mesaba,* and *Californian.* (Thanks to John Booth and the Booth Titanic Signal Archive, many of these messages, and others occurring before, during, and after the sinking, have been preserved.) Most of these ice warnings were acknowledged and some posted. Any of the ship's officers who understood their meaning must have realized that entry into ice-infested waters was inevitable. It seems likely that the first sighting of ice would have resulted in the ship curbing her speed. In an ironic way this was the case. After Fred Fleet's call to First Officer Murdoch on the bridge, "Iceberg right ahead," the *Titanic*'s efforts to steer clear were accompanied by the reversal of her engines, a decision later said to have impeded her capacity to maneuver quickly. Thus the first ice the *Titanic* sighted was the last.

What I am implying is that, prior to the *Titanic* disaster and especially during the first decade of wireless, seamen put supreme trust in the visual verification of phenomena. Wireless messages about a hazard such as icebergs were often less a call to action than a call to greater vigilance. Given the presence of ice in her route, the *Titanic* could have slowed down or changed to a more southerly course and even speeded up. She did neither, but preferred to wait and *see* before acting. This suggests that prior to the sinking, when large companies like the White Star Line routed their vessels, wireless played a supplemental rather than a determining role.

Another aspect of this maritime communications drama concerns the ice warning the *Titanic* received at 10:30 P.M. on 13 April from the Furness Withy ship, *Rappahannock*, wherein wireless was not the medium. Using Morse lamp as she passed the *Titanic*, the *Rappahannock*, eastbound out of Halifax, told the *Titanic* of the icefield ahead and that in negotiating it the *Rappahannock* had damaged her rudder. First Officer Murdoch acknowledged the message, but still held to the previous course and speed.

The last ice warning the *Titanic* received—partially received would be more accurate—came from the *Californian* at 11 P.M. It precipitated a debate that still rages over where that ship was located with respect to the *Titanic* and what its captain, Stanley Lord, should or should not have done in the hours that followed.

The wireless side of the story begins with the relatively inexperienced operator on the *Californian*, Cyril Evans, age 20, starting to send the aforementioned message indicating the presence of ice. He signaled that it had caused the *Californian* to shut down her engines and drift for the night. Phillips was at the key working Cape Race (Newfoundland) when Evans's transmission intruded. Since the *Californian* was five to twenty miles away—the exact distance is still debated—her signal was loud, clear, and an unwelcome interruption. Phillips responded with, "Keep out! Shut up! You're jamming my signal. I'm working Cape Race." Evans did not try again. He turned off his equipment and went to bed a short time later, within minutes of the *Titanic's* fatal collision.

According to British maritime historian Geoffrey Marcus, blame for the failure of Evans's message to be acknowledged resides with both the young operator and with Captain Lord. Marcus argues that what Evans should have done was to send a formal Master's Service Message (MSG). Phillips might have then replied to it, or at least put him on hold, since an MSG necessitated a response. As it was, Evans sent an unofficial dispatch. For his part, Captain Lord should have insisted on an answer, even if the initial dispatch was unofficial, since he had suggested that Evans send it. In defense of Evans and Lord, it should be noted that the reason they signaled the *Titanic* about their predicament was partly due to the knowledge that the ship was nearby and worth contacting. Although an MSG would have been judicious, the presence of ice in the region was common knowledge to any vessel with wireless.

Marcus also contends that Evans should have stayed at his post and not retired for the night, since "emergency conditions" prevailed. Perhaps. Yes there was ice, but the sea was calm and the air clear. Furthermore, Evans was the only operator on board and, like Phillips, he had put in a long day, longer than the seamen who worked eight-hour shifts or those on watch who served four. Normal sign-off time for a station having one operator was 11 P.M.; Evans had already overstayed it by half-an-hour. As Senator Smith would discover during the American inquiry, Marconi operators were overworked as well as underpaid.

John Booth and Sean Coughlan, in their excellent analysis of *Titanic* related wireless messages, suggest that this infamous information gap between the *Titanic* and *Californian* can be blamed partly on maritime law, regulated in this case by the British Board of Trade. Normal safety precautions, such as the maintenance of a twenty-four–hour watch, were not extended to include wireless. As a result, the divided loyalty of wireless operators, between messages relating to navigation and private dispatches from which the Marconi Company made most of its profits, was generally unquestioned. We might also add that some culpability for the "*Californian* incident" is also due the Marconi Company. Given the near tragedy of the *Republic*, they could have developed more efficient procedures for ship stations with only one operator.

What happened on the *Californian* after Evans went to sleep compounded the problem and has given the ship an unsought immortality. In the distance loomed another vessel, her lights clearly visible. Was it the *Titanic*? Was the *Californian* the nearby ship several of the *Titanic*'s officers observed? Was there a third ship in the vicinity? Other books have grappled in exhaustive detail with these enduring questions. For the purposes of a wireless-based assessment, we should note the following sequence of events. At 12:15 A.M. Third Officer Groves, on his way to bed after his watch was relieved, stopped off at the Marconi cabin. He knew some Morse code and put on the headphones but did not know how to start, or more precisely to wind up, the magnetic detector that powered the transmitter. Rather than further disturb an already half-asleep Evans, he abandoned the idea of a late-night listening session, and in so doing almost certainly missed hearing the *Titanic*'s distress call.

The nearby ship, which had also been noticed by Captain Lord before he retired, was now of interest to the new watch, Second Officer Stone. He signaled her using Morse lamp. No answer. Eight white rockets were sighted (the

Titanic fired eight while in her death throes). Captain Lord was informed of the rockets via the speaking tube. He asked their color and if they were company signals (white was for distress, but company signals, which employed a variety of colors, could also use it). Stone replied that he did not know if they were company signals but was trying to establish contact by Morse lamp. He was told to keep on Morsing. At 2 A.M. the ship appeared to steam away. Stone sent an apprentice, Gibson, to inform the captain. Then he did so himself via the speaking tube forty-five minutes later.

Despite the unusual events of the evening, no one had the presence of mind to wake Evans and bring wireless into the investigation—no one, that is, until Chief Officer Stewart came on watch at 4 A.M. When informed by Stone of what had been happening he roused Evans, who quickly found out about the tragedy. The *Californian* arrived on the scene several hours later as the *Carpathia* was picking up the remaining survivors. It turned out to be a case of "better never than late," given what happened when word about the *Californian's* earlier inaction broke in the press and was later pursued at the American and British inquiries.

The *Californian* incident, and the literature it has spawned, continues to divide *Titanic* scholarship into at least three factions: those who think that Captain Lord was negligent; those, sometimes known as Lordites, who argue that he has been a scapegoat, unfairly maligned for acting in ways that were not inconsistent with maritime practice in 1912; and those who contend that neither case has been sufficiently proven. Most in the latter two categories have favored a formal and comprehensive re-examination of all the facts of the case, a courtesy denied Captain Lord in 1912 and one which he sought until his death in 1962 at the age of eighty-four. In 1992 the case was reopened by a British maritime tribunal. Captain Lord was exonerated of the charge that he failed to respond to a ship in distress, but held accountable for not fully investigating the distress rockets.

When Phillips snubbed the *Californian's* transmission, he had been at work for sixteen hours repairing the apparatus and clearing the backlog of messages. Several hours earlier he had received a dispatch from the *Mesaba* reporting "much heavy pack ice and a great number large icebergs" at coordinates close to the *Titanic's* position. He acknowledged the message. The *Mesaba's* operator stood by for an acknowledgment from Captain Smith, whom he assumed would be immediately privy to the information. It never came. Phillips put the dispatch under a paperweight and continued working Cape Race to reduce the backlog of private messages. Exhausted and impatient by this time, perhaps he forgot about the priority due navigational dispatches. A more likely, though purely speculative reason for his inaction, might have been the belief that, despite its importance, similar messages had been coming in all day and were delivered to the bridge. What Phillips must have failed to realize was how close the coordinates of latitude and longitude in the *Mesaba*'s ice warning were to the *Titanic*'s position; given the ship's course and speed, she would be there before his shift was over at midnight.

When Bride joined Phillips for the shift change, Phillips remarked that they must have struck something. Captain Smith soon entered the Marconi cabin and told them about the collision. He said the damage was being assessed and to stand by to send a call for assistance. Not believing the ship vulnerable, the two operators joked about the situation. Ten minutes later the captain returned and told them to transmit. Phillips began sending CQD. Bride suggested he also try SOS: "It's the new call and it may be your last chance to send it." Popular tradition, and many commentaries, often cite this as the first SOS in maritime history. It was not. Although the *Titanic* may have been the first British ship to use SOS, continental European vessels had already employed it. Earlier that month the call was used by the French liner *Niagara* when she was damaged in the same region for the same reasons.

With the *Titanic*'s plight looking more desperate each minute, her distress call did not go unheeded. Unfortunately, given the rate at which she was succumbing, the only ship close enough to attempt a rescue of the numerous passengers for whom there was no lifeboat space was the *Californian*. The first response to Phillip's call came from the *Frankfurt*. Her operator took the message to the captain. The signal also reached Cape Race. Their reaction was one of disbelief, followed by shock when repeated transmissions confirmed the worst. Numerous ships eventually formed a network of recipients, among them the *Caronia, Mount Temple, Yipiranga, Cincinnati, Celtic, Baltic, Olympic, Birma, Virginian, Asian,* and most notably the *Carpathia*, which was fifty-eight miles southeast of the *Titanic*. Given her position and top speed, she was the vessel that could get there quickest.

What happened with the *Carpathia* and her wireless operator, Harold Cottam, contrasts with the situation of Evans and the *Californian*. Cottam (age 22), the only operator on board, was preparing to turn in for the night. He decided to linger at the headphones awhile longer to get news of the coal strike in England. During his shift he had picked up several ice warnings, including the one the *Californian* tried to send to the *Titanic*. Cottam took off the headphones and started to undress, thereby missing the *Titanic*'s initial CQD SOS. Then he put them on again to ask the *Titanic* if she knew that messages were being held for her at Cape Cod, and was greeted by the distress call. Cottam quickly informed the captain, Arthur Rostron, of the *Titanic*'s plight and position.

Rostron reacted decisively. He fired his ship to full speed in the direction of the disaster and prepared her facilities for a rescue at sea. The *Carpathia* arrived on the scene shortly after 4 A.M. and gathered unto her what remained of the *Titanic*'s passengers and crew. It was a courageous effort, one that earned Rostron the Congressional Medal of Honor. It was also a calculated risk and fraught with danger, since the *Carpathia* had to maneuver through an ice field lethal enough to give her a share of the *Titanic*'s fate.

With the *Carpathia* on the way, Phillips kept signaling. News of the *Titanic*'s plight ricocheted around the North Atlantic. The London *Times* would later liken the scenario to a great wounded animal summoning help from its kin. Most respondents tried to help in whatever way they could, and a number of ships altered course to come to the *Titanic*'s aid. However, the magnitude of the disaster was not clearly understood by all who received the distress call. The *Olympic* asked if the *Titanic* was steering a course to meet them. Phillips patiently stated MGY's circumstances and was in turn notified that the *Olympic* was headed toward them at full steam. But she was an agonizingly distant 500 miles.

Another misconstrued interpretation of the distress call came from the first ship to receive it, the *Frankfurt*. When she re-established contact it was without a sense of the urgency of the situation. She asked, "What is the matter?" Whereupon Captain Smith was supposed to have said, "That man is a fool." We do know what Phillips tapped back as his response: "You fool. Stand by and keep out." Since the *Frankfurt* was a Telefunken ship, this seems like a case of the old wireless rivalry resurfacing, compounded by the competition and tension between two nations who would shortly be at war. The incident became newsworthy just over a week later. Germany cited it as a gross example of British inefficiency at sea, and Senator Smith saw it as yet another example of the questionable way Marconi Marine conducted its business.

The *Titanic*'s wireless functioned almost to the end. The drama of the last few minutes in the Marconi cabin was recounted by Bride at the American Inquiry and has become one of the enduring legends of that infamous night. Here is a brief summary:

Phillips keeps signaling. The captain enters and releases the operators under the "Everyman for himself" declaration. Phillips will not let go of the key. Bride fastens a lifebelt to him. A crewman enters the cabin and tries to steal it. They dispatch him in a way that has never been made clear—nor was it of sufficient concern to Senator Smith to explore further when he had Bride on the stand. With water almost to the level of the Marconi cabin as the *Titanic* descends by the bow, the power fades to nil. Phillips and Bride leave and eventually wind up in the water. They are pulled aboard lifeboats. (Phillips'

presence in a lifeboat has been doubted by later commetators.) Phillips dies of
exposure exacerbated by exhaustion and is later resurrected as one of the enduring heroes of the disaster. Bride survives to narrate the harrowing events in
an exclusive interview with the *New York Times*.

As the *Carpathia* steamed to New York with the survivors the world became
privy to news of the disaster but not the details. Newspaper accounts ranged
from the *New York Times*'s somber estimate that 1,250 had perished to the
New York Sun's report that all had been saved. By 18 April the former estimate, the one nobody wanted to believe, turned out to be closer to the truth;
agonizingly closer, since the actual number of fatalities now appeared to ex-
ceed 1,500. The confused reporting resulted from the way the two Harolds,
Cottam and Bride, handled communications from the *Carpathia*, and the way
transmissions from a variety of sources were interpreted.

Cottam began sending the names of survivors shortly after they were taken
on board and made comfortable. Given the limited range of his apparatus, he
had to relay the list to the *Olympic*. The list was forwarded to Cape Race and
then directed to New York by wire as well as by wireless. An exhausted Cottam was soon assisted by Bride, who, recovering from exposure as well as a
leg injury, had to be carried to the Marconi cabin. They worked tirelessly and,
as it turned out, conspiratorially. All requests for further information—from
the press, the White Star Line, President Taft, and even Marconi at the urging
of the United States government—went unheeded. On 15 April the following
message to the International Mercantile Marine Company was composed by
the *Titanic*'s most notorious survivor, Bruce Ismay, chairman of the White
Star Line: "Deeply regret advise you *Titanic* sank this morning after collision
with iceberg, resulting in serious loss of life." According to Captain Rostron,
who Senator Smith contacted about the incident, the message was given to
the purser, who took it immediately to the Marconi Cabin. It was not sent
until 17 April.

When Ismay was somewhat recovered he drafted another dispatch, which
was sent without delay, also on 17 April. It was signed "YAMSI," a personal
code reversing the letters of his name: "Most desireable Titanic crew aboard
Carpathia should be returned home earliest moment possible. Suggest you
hold *Cedric* sailing her daylight Friday." This request was perhaps motivated
by both a concern for crew and a desire to leave the United States before all
hell broke loose. It was one of three messages proposing such action. They
were intercepted by the U.S. Navy and forwarded to Senator Smith, who
made sure what was intended did not come to pass.

Responsibility for what was sent from the *Carpathia*, and whether messages
received were acted upon or not, was in the hands of Cottam and Bride, with

Bride having seniority. Several factors can be invoked to explain their behavior. The two most compelling are loyalty to the Marconi Company and its business associates, such as White Star, and thoughts that the two operators might have entertained to profit personally from their experiences by giving as yet undisclosed testimony to the press upon arrival in New York. At the American inquiry, they defended their actions by insisting that the American operators who were sending the inquiries, often non-Marconi Navy men, could not use continental Morse code properly. It was also claimed that it was not Marconi practice to send important or official transmissions via a relay using other ships—this was given in defense of their failure to send Ismay's first message, which was conceived when the *Carpathia* was too far at sea to reach any shore station with her equipment. And finally, they noted how, since they were under so much pressure, Captain Rostron told them to handle only "official" messages and those relating to the survivors.

Senator Smith soon found out that the first two reasons could not be supported conclusively. Navy operators, although not stellar at the apparatus, were competent enough to send to and receive from those in the employ of Marconi. As to the second reason, Marconi Marine had no official policy prohibiting the relay of important dispatches, save the lingering influence of the nointercommunications rule, which would discourage but not necessarily prohibit the use of other wireless companies in such a relay.

The final reason Cottam and Bride gave for their failure to release more information, that they were following Captain Rostron's orders, was, to Smith's mind, taking a suggestion too literally in order to cover ulterior motives. Later questioning of Captain Rostron indicated that he did support the sending of official messages, along with survivors' names and information, by the "most convenient means." Several intercepted dispatches to the *Carpathia* before she docked indicate possible reasons for Cottam and Bride being retentive communicators.

The first was, "Say old man Marconi Company taking good care of you. Keep your mouth shut and hold your story. It is fixed so you will get big money." It was followed by, "Arranged for your exclusive story for dollars in four figures. Mr. Marconi agreeing. Say nothing until you see me." Both were signed by Frederick Sammis, Marconi's chief engineer in New York. They were sent on 18 April as the *Carpathia* was about to dock, thus encouraging but not causing a strategy Cottam and Bride had already adopted. Whatever prompted them to be less than thorough operators following the disaster—perhaps they were inspired by Jack Binns of the *Republic*, who turned misfortune into a fortune—now seemed to be sanctioned by their own commander-in-chief.

Senator Smith put Marconi and Sammis on the stand. Marconi denied ordering the messages, but conceded he knew about the planned exclusive and the payment involved. Sammis took responsibility for the messages, but claimed that the wording transmitted differed from his original. Nevertheless, he defended his intent with a reference to picking up the spirits of the operators.

The Senator then got to the heart of the matter by following a series of revealing facts. Marconi had a business arrangement with the *New York Times* that dated from 1907; it provided the paper with an exclusive transAtlantic news link. He was also one of the few VIPs allowed on board the *Carpathia* after she landed, at a time when the press was kept dockside. When Marconi boarded he took with him Jim Speers of the *Times*, with the full advice and assistance of Carr Van Anda, the managing editor of the *Times*. Bride dictated his riveting account to Speers. Cottam left the ship and made his way to the nearby Strand Hotel, where the *Times* had set up temporary facilities, and gave his version of the *Carpathia's* role in the disaster. It was a major scoop for the paper and an embarrassment for Marconi when the persistent Senator made the famous inventor's actions public.

According to Wyn Craig Wade, who has made a thorough study of the role of the Michigan Senator in the American inquiry, Smith pursued the popular inventor with zeal. When Marconi commented that the money paid Bride ($1,000) and Cottam ($750) for their stories was a just reward for heroic work, the outspoken Senator suggested that he pay them a decent wage. Smith used the interrogation of Marconi as a platform for his crusade against the way monopolies and trusts often violate the public interest. He found the practices of the Marconi Company cavalier and self-serving, although he was somewhat more forgiving of the Marconi operators and the *New York Times*. Despite Smith's belief that Marconi was lying and evasive when questioned, pressure from other committee members and the public's adoration of the inventor prevented him from going as far as he wanted to in his exposé. He settled for a statement from Marconi discouraging any future attempt on the part of his operators to withhold information so it could be later sold in an exclusive manner.

The journalistic piecing together of the story of the sinking, as the *Carpathia* headed for New York, became an exercise in creative news making utilizing a small number of not always consistent wireless messages; most had to be relayed three or four times, adding to the confusion. This was the case at some point on 15 April, when the news everyone wanted to hear—a transmission stating the *Titanic* was safe and in tow to Halifax—became the basis of several headlines, including one in the venerable *New York Evening Sun*. A train was even chartered to go from New York to Halifax and retrieve the passengers. The next day confirmation of the worst forced its return.

A plausible explanation for this misleading message soon emerged. Somehow an operator spliced together an inquiry asking if the *Titanic* and her passengers were safe with information sent several times that night by the *Asian*, indicating she was towing an oil tanker to Halifax; another interpretation of the transmission had the *Virginian* doing the towing. At the time, amateur operators were thought to be responsible, and the weight of *Titanic* scholarship still favors this view. However, it is possible that a commercial operator receiving signals at the limits of reception or transmission, who would be naturally biased toward the believable rather than unthinkable, might have transcribed and forwarded such a message.

From 15–18 April, amidst the fragmentary and sporadic transmissions and the activity of numerous stations, an unlikely location emerged as an important source for late-breaking news: Wanamaker's department store in New York. This was because of the enterprise of its young Marconi man, a Russian-Jewish immigrant named David Sarnoff (1891–1971). For a small but influential coterie of journalists, Wanamaker's became the disaster's nerve center—a 1912 version of "mission control." It also provided a launching pad for Sarnoff's unprecedented career in broadcast media.

5

Sarnoff's Luck

Sarnoff began at Wanamaker's two years before the *Titanic* entered his life. It was nearly a short-lived assignment. In his previous wireless posting at Siasconset (Massachusetts), he had been instrumental in relaying the distress call and organizing a rescue when the airship *Vaniman* ran into trouble. A new *Vaniman* was launched shortly after Sarnoff started at Wanamaker's and he volunteered to serve as wireless operator for an early test flight. Several transportation snags between New York and Atlantic City prevented him from arriving before the *Vaniman* took off. It crashed and burned killing all on board. This incident contributed to the legend of "Sarnoff's luck"—his ability to be in the right place at the right time . . . or, in this instance, perhaps we should say, "the wrong place at the right time."

Throughout his life, Sarnoff had the prescient ability to turn unexpected challenges into opportunities. This would eventually lead him to an eminence in the field of electronic mass media that in many ways paralleled what Henry Ford achieved in the realm of the automobile. Entry into this domain began with one such challenge. In 1906 Sarnoff was an ambitious but nervous fifteen-year-old when he trekked into the *New York Herald* building determined to begin a career in the newspaper business. Unperturbed by the thought of starting at the bottom, he asked the man behind the window in the lobby for a job, any job. He soon found out he was in the outer office of the Commercial Cable Company, not the *New York Herald*. With telegraph keys clicking hypnotically in the background he was offered a job as messenger boy for five dollars a week. Intrigued by the opportunity and the unusual work environment, he duly accepted. Subsequently, and largely on his own, he learned

Morse code and acquired a practice telegraph. Within a year he had a job with the Marconi Wireless Telegraph Company of America, where his prowess at the key became legendary.

Before the Marconi Company offered Sarnoff the position of manager of their Wanamaker facilities, he was assigned to the shore stations of Siasconset and Sea Gate (New York). During this time he also had brief but significant experience as a shipboard operator. While serving these assignments, he read all the literature he could dealing with the nature and application of the wireless. Eventually, he had several meetings with the titan of this technology, the legendary Marconi, whom young Sarnoff regarded with awe and respect. Although neither could realize it at the time, the next decade would see them become firm friends, with the younger man ascending to his own niche of renown.

Sarnoff's strategic moment at Wanamaker's, when he relayed news of the plight of the *Titanic* to a desperate public, became an oft-recalled aspect of his career. It was also an event he was known to over-embellish and distort for the sake of self-promotion. How it began has never been completely clear. Most accounts say he was at his post when he picked up the *Titanic*'s distress signal via a relay from her sister ship the *Olympic*. Sarnoff always insisted this was the case, most notably in a statement about the incident, which became the subject of a later article in the *Saturday Evening Post*.

Two recent commentators see it differently. In a respectful and tempered biography, Carl Dreher argues that Sarnoff could not have been at Wanamaker's that night (Sunday) and, even if he was, that the wireless signals from the *Titanic* and *Olympic* would not have been strong enough to reach New York. Dreher's alternative scenario has Sarnoff somehow getting word of the event, perhaps through a newspaper extra, and *then* going to his station to see if he could be of help; a similar view is expressed by Tom Lewis in his book *Empire of the Air*, which became the basis of Ken Burns's evocative 1992 PBS documentary of the same name. What happened at Wanamaker's after Sarnoff donned the earphones, however, can be accounted for with more certainty.

The first conclusive signals Sarnoff received came from the *Olympic*. He made contact with her and notified the press. Reporters came. So did store employees, relatives and friends of the passengers, and a mélange of the curious. Eventually, the police had to be called in to prevent a secondary disaster at Wanamaker's, which was rapidly becoming a secondary news story as a result of coverage by reporters working for William Randolf Hearst.

Fueled by coffee and donuts, Sarnoff stayed at his post for three days and three nights, a performance that reminded many of young Jack Binns's role in the rescue of the *Republic* three years earlier. By Wednesday, the 17th, the airwaves were plagued with interference. The Marconi Company decided to shut down most of its Northeast operations, and the Wanamaker's apparatus had to cease in deference to several of the company's more primary stations, such as the head office on William Street.

The news Sarnoff—and two assistants he omits in later recollections—received was dismal: no details regarding the sinking, only the names of survivors, far fewer names than anyone had expected; then, slowly and inexorably, the names of assumed casualties. After the shutdown, with the *Carpathia* approaching New York, the entourage at Wanamaker's dispersed. Many headed dockside. Sarnoff took a short break for a Turkish rub at the Astor Hotel on Lower Broadway, compliments of Vincent Astor, who had been at Sarnoff's side when news confirming that John Jacob Astor, Vincent's father, was not among the survivors. Sarnoff emerged from the hotel refreshed but still tired, and made his way to Sea Gate station to see if there was anything more he could do. Little remained. Wireless had done its job and the press now descended on the *Carpathia*. Mission accomplished, Sarnoff, who was emotionally as well as physically exhausted, went home and slept for twenty-four hours. He would later observe: "It seemed as if the whole anxious world was attached to those phones."

In ancient times, a messenger relaying the kind of unfortunate news that was Sarnoff's burden might have found himself in jeopardy. But since the dawn of the electric age and the accompanying rise of the mass media, almost any information about an event is preferable to uncertainty. Sarnoff became the exalted messenger for a company that rose in esteem and affluence as a result of the *Titanic* disaster. His fortunes did likewise. By the end of the year he became chief inspector for Marconi facilities throughout the country. After World War I, American Marconi was taken over by General Electric, which called its new subsidiary the Radio Corporation of America. Sarnoff thrived in the new order and became RCA's general manager in 1926, guiding that company's destiny over the next four decades. Throughout his rise he often noted how the *Titanic* disaster "brought radio to the front, and incidentally, me."

Before leaving Marconi for RCA, Sarnoff wrote a prophetic memo. In November 1916, he proposed turning one of radio's greatest liabilities—access to private point-to-point messages by anyone with adequate equipment tuned to the wavelength in use—into a powerful asset. He proposed the "Radio Music Box," a radio receiver to be located in living rooms and parlors, which would employ loudspeakers rather than earphones to bring music and voice to a wide public. His superiors were uninterested. Perhaps their attitude reflected Marconi's persistent belief at this time that radio was, and should only be, a medium for telegraphic rather than for vocal or musical communication. Ten years later broadcast radio as an information and entertainment medium would be a reality. Although Sarnoff and RCA were not first in this endeavor, they eventually became major players in a collective effort that involved several interest groups and companies.

6

Reassessment and Regulation

The sinking of the *Titanic* demonstrated that nothing in the realm of transportation and communication could or should be taken for granted. Wireless was now deemed indispensable and in need of regulatory policies appropriate to the role it played in the movement of information and people. Previously, attitudes about how to control the new medium had been ambivalent.

In the years leading up to the *Titanic* disaster, the general public regarded wireless with a mixture of awe and indifference. It was awesome when a heart-stopping event, such as the sinking of the *Republic*, thrust the technology and those associated with it into the media spotlight. Apart from these visible moments, in its normal day-to-day, year-to-year operations, wireless was often taken for granted. Although Marconi was widely known, the success of his commercial ventures only occasionally equaled the renown of his name. Not until 1910 would his empire be solidly in the black to stay.

During this early period there was little call for regulation on the part of the press. Most newspapers seemed content to wait for the next wireless event or hero. While the sinking of the *Titanic* inherited this expectation, it did so with a difference, particularly when news broke about the inaction of the *Californian*. On one hand, the press regarded wireless as having performed up to all previous expectations; on the other, it suggested that with better monitoring the medium might have helped save more lives.

The attitude among those interest groups who were closest to and most dependent on wireless during its first decade—governments and shipping and insurance companies—favored increased regulation. As mentioned before, their concerns led to international conferences in Madrid (1903) and Berlin

(1906), which considered the nointercommunications policy of the Marconi company, the licensing of stations and operators, and the establishment of an international distress call and procedure. The fate of the *Titanic* showed that more sweeping aspects of wireless practice had to be regulated, among them the range of the apparatus, its power source, the hours a station should be operative, and the allocation of frequencies.

In the United States, some of these concerns had already been raised in Congress, but pre-*Titanic* wireless regulation was minimal. The most important policy measure was the Wireless Ship Act of June 1910, which took effect July in 1911. It was a reaction to the increasing passenger volume on North Atlantic routes and an attempt to frame an American response to the conventions established in Madrid and Berlin. The bill stipulated that all oceangoing steamships using U.S. ports, carrying fifty or more passengers, and traveling to destinations 200 or more miles apart, must carry an "efficient apparatus" for radiotelegraphic communication and a "skilled operator." It also required the equipment to have a daytime range of at least 100 miles and made intercommunication compulsory. No provisions were established regarding what constituted a "skilled operator," the frequencies to be used and by whom, or the amount of time a station was to remain on the air.

The Wireless Ship Act pressed home to legislators lessons learned from the *Republic*, but her fate would have impressed them more had a major tragedy ensued. What if Jack Binns had been incapacitated, with no one else capable sending a distress call, or suppose he had only been able to render his call for a few minutes and someone at the receiving end had dismissed it as another amateur hoax?

At least some farsighted legislators must have been thinking along these lines. A House of Representatives report from 1910 prophetically noted that without further and more specific wireless regulation a major disaster might occur. Thoughts such as this led to the circulation of six bills in 1910 and thirteen in 1912 prior to the fateful events of April. But the Wireless Ship Act was as far as the government was willing to go, and even that act was violated on numerous occasions when Marconi operators followed the nointercommunications policy and snubbed transmissions from American companies such as United Wireless and Lee De Forest.

Why was the call for legislation not more emphatic? In part because this was still the age of classical capitalism. Antiregulatory lobbies were a fact of American political life. In the case of wireless policy, which began to be debated in the press in 1910, the opposition invoked such sacred tenets of American ideology as free enterprise, free speech, and property rights—i.e., ownership of the airwaves above a transmitter on land that the sender either owned or leased.

The situation in Britain was not dissimilar. A bill proposing the mandatory use of wireless on oceangoing ships carrying fifty or more passengers was tabled in the House of Commons in 1910. It was prompted by concerns about safety and navigation, and defeated on the grounds that it would be a further expense to shipping companies and thus hinder competitiveness. Doubtlessly, the intense Anglo-German rivalry for Maritime supremacy weighed on the minds of many legislators.

In the United States, the antiregulatory position was occasionally vulnerable to challenge as a result of the actions of amateur operators, who were starting to become a major nuisance to commercial and military interests. Marconi wanted to see them contained, but he preferred to put up with the situation rather than support regulatory policy that might result in the passage of bills so inclusive they might affect the way he managed his operations. In the pages of the *New York Times* he occasionally voiced his opposition to what worried legislators were conjuring.

In the aftermath of the *Titanic* disaster, Marconi modified his position on wireless regulation, but his new outlook remained self-serving. His views appeared in an "Authorized Interview" in the June 2, 1912, issue of the *World's Work*. There is no indication of the exact date of this interview, or when it occurred with respect to the American inquiry, which began 19 April, or the British, which started 2 May.

Marconi urged that a major lesson of the disaster was the necessity of having two wireless operators on an oceangoing vessel. The *Carpathia*, he noted, picked up the *Titanic*'s distress signal by the "merest accident"; he made no mention of the *Californian* incident. Either it had not been discussed in the press or at the inquiries at the time of the interview; or it is also possible that Marconi wanted to refrain from entering the controversy. In reaffirming his opposition to broad regulatory changes, he went on to consider the notorious nointercommunications policy. He argued that it should only be prohibited in the case of urgent messages in the CQD or SOS category: "Beyond such regulations and those bearing on the loss of vessels and lives, I hardly think it feasible for international agreements to go." It is remarkable here, in light of the events surrounding the sinking of the *Titanic*, that he did not affirm the necessity of specific intercommunications relating to navigation—ice warnings, for example.

And what about those pesky amateurs? On this subject Marconi was much less committed to an antiregulatory position. He called for stringent policies whereby the government would tighten the licensing procedure for wireless operators, limit amateurs to a specific wavelength, and impose stiff fines for interference. Part of his rationale was the belief that amateurs were responsible for the composite message about the *Titanic* being damaged and on her way to Halifax with all passengers safe, which was never conclusively proven, however. The interview ended with Marconi confessing pride and gratification at having played a role in the rescue, and promising to take steps to improve wireless equipment by increasing its range.

No one felt the need for wireless regulation following the *Titanic* disaster more acutely than Michigan Senator William Alden Smith, who led the American inquiry. Although Smith was a Republican, his populist leanings and frequent criticism of the monopolistic power of large trusts did not often endear him to his party's old and still powerful elite. He saw Marconi as engaging in corporate practices not always in the public interest. Smith was irked by the failure of the *Carpathia's* Marconi man, Harold Cottam, and Harold Bride, the operator who had survived the *Titanic's* sinking, to forward more information about the disaster.

Marconi's testimony about the incident deepened Smith's suspicions about the way the "big business" of wireless conducted its affairs. A Marconi operator's first loyalty seemed to be to the Marconi company, not to the ship's captain, the shipping line, or government officials. Smith kept implying the need for more comprehensive wireless regulations during his questioning of those involved in this aspect of the disaster. His closing summation contained an impassioned plea for legislation to bring it about.

The initial public response to the role of wireless in the disaster was largely positive. Marconi, along with the *Titanic's* deceased operator, Jack Phillips, were given heroic treatment in the press at a time when heroes were sorely needed. The sentiments expressed in a speech by the British postmaster general on 18 April summed up the attitude of many people on both sides of the Atlantic (with the possible exception of Senator Smith): "Those who had been saved had been saved by one man—Mr. Marconi." Among the American accolades was a telegram from Thomas Edison, who had publicly endorsed Marconi's abilities a few years earlier.

To be celebrated in this way was perhaps the high point of Marconi's career. The invention that for over a decade had been linked to his name was now synonymous with it. Unprecedented business opportunities followed. The question marks clouding his reputation, particularly the "all safe on *Titanic*" wireless message and his later collusion with the *New York Times*, would soon be forgotten.

Because wireless had at least performed up to previous expectations, its practitioners were spared admonishment. Marconi was critiqued rather than criticized, and advised on how a good thing could be made better.

The call for wireless regulation in the press and at the two inquiries, was more tempered than the one dealing with shipping and navigational practice. In the latter arena, outrage was expressed over the frequent practice of large liners, with fewer lifeboat spaces than passengers, steaming rapidly at night through regions where ice was present. Here, the White Star Line was chastised for doing what was often done by other companies.

In the wake of Senator Smith's inquiry, the U.S. government had no intention of waiting over a year for a new international wireless convention to make policy changes. In July, President Taft signed into law an amendment to the 1910 Wireless Ship Act. Vessels covered by the original act described earlier now had to have two operators on duty so the station could function twenty-four hours a day, and an auxiliary power source. Also in July, a sweeping bill was passed, the Radio Act, which became law the following December.

The Radio Act required all operators to be licensed, with the Secretary of Labor and Commerce in charge of the procedure. Stations now had to have a specific transmitter capacity and adhere to a particular wavelength. The amateurs, who had been heroic figures a few years earlier, were now out of favor with government, the wireless companies, and, because of what allegedly happened with some of the *Titanic*'s transmissions, the press. They were still permitted to listen in—something that would be difficult to prevent in any case—but could only obtain a license to transmit using the shortwave part of the radio spectrum.

Susan Douglas, in her excellent history of the early years of American broadcasting, refers to these amateurs, now limited to shortwave transmission, as being "exiled to an ethereal reservation." And so it must have seemed at the time. Although Marconi's initial experiments used shortwave, he thought it had limited potential for long-distance transmission. Long low-frequency wavelengths seemed to work better, especially in following the curvature of the earth over saltwater; they also required an increase in power proportional to the distance to be covered. Going with what worked, rather than reflecting on what might be theoretically possible, Marconi committed himself to the longwave/high-power strategy. Others followed his lead.

By 1920, however, he was forced to re-evaluate this commitment. Amateurs were achieving extraordinary results communicating over great distances using shortwave and low power. Douglas's "ethereal reservation" was becoming a small-scale version of McLuhan's "global village." A theoretical explanation emerged when Arthur Kennelly in the United States and Oliver Heaviside in England explained the role of the ionosphere in reflecting radio waves back to earth. Short wavelengths are exceptionally efficient exploiters of this property, and, after 1920, Marconi committed himself to using them to develop radio's potential for international communication on a global scale.

The Radio Act also established new procedures for distress calls, in part to prevent the type of confusion that plagued some of the *Titanic*'s last transmissions. A distress frequency was established, and when it was being used all ships and shore stations unable to assist directly or relay the message were to cease signaling. In addition, shore stations had to monitor this frequency every fifteen minutes for two minutes. SOS was deemed to be the official distress call—any reluctance to use it, instead of CQD, had by this time been erased by the notoriety given SOS by the *Titanic*. And, to keep amateur operators from interfering with or faking such transmissions, the right to impose heavy fines and suspend their licenses was made law.

Marconi was not unappreciative of the positive benefits to him of the regulations of the Radio Act. It would be easier for his large company to implement them than for smaller rivals. However, over the next several years, another legacy of Senator Smith would pursue him, as it would Western Union and the American Telephone and Telegraph Company: antitrust legislation.

The Radio Act also conceded more to the military than must have been to Marconi's liking. A wide part of the radio spectrum was reserved for the Navy, and provisions were made for them to upgrade equipment and extend their jurisdiction. Private stations could now be closed down or taken over should conditions warrant, which is what came to pass with the United States's entry into World War I in 1917. This set the stage for the postwar takeover of American Marconi by General Electric through their subsidiary RCA.

The quick action on the part of American legislators following the *Titanic* disaster influenced the proceedings of the International Conference for the Safety of Life at Sea held in London between 12 November 1913 and 20 January 1914. Policies were implemented affecting lifeboats, navigational procedures in hazardous conditions, the establishment of an international ice patrol, and communications. To prevent a recurrence of what happened with the *Californian*, all rockets were deemed to be distress signals and had to be responded to accordingly. Although oceangoing ships had to carry a wireless with sufficient range and an auxiliary power source, the American requirement of two operators was waived in the case of certain freighters, where a member of the crew competent enough to decipher an emergency transmission could substitute for the second operator.

A total of seventy-four articles were signed into agreement by the thirteen nations who participated in the London Conference. The measures pertaining to wireless did not go as far as the American Radio Act, but the desired results were achieved. Since the *Titanic* perished in 1912, no oceangoing vessel using the Atlantic shipping lanes has been lost because of a collision with ice. The London Conference unequivocally showed that maritime communication had come a long way from the kind of incident that befell the Collins liner *Pacific* in 1856: months after she disappeared without a trace, a message in a bottle drifted to the Hebrides. It described the ship going down surrounded by icebergs.

Part III

CHASING THE STORY

Real news is bad news—bad news *about* somebody, or bad news *for* somebody.

—Marshall McLuhan, *Understanding Media*

What makes the sinking of the Titanic such an impressive episode in the history of twentieth-century journalism is its duration. Like the Kennedy assassination, the *Titanic* disaster was front-page news for several weeks throughout North America and parts of Europe, and it lingered for at least several days in many of the rest of the world's papers. Using this criterion, the story that stands just behind it in longevity (apart from war related coverage) is the Lindbergh baby kidnapping, not the epoch-making flight. It held the front page longer, and unlike the flight, was an important item in the newspapers of countries not favorably disposed toward the United States. By contrast, the recent O. J. Simpson so-called "Trial of the Century," although a major and prolonged American media event, has had only periodic global interest.

News about the plight of the *Titanic* circulated with a rapidity unmatched by any previous event. It set a journalistic precedent, one that would be redeployed during the great upheaval of World War I. Seventy-five years of instantaneous electric communication came to the fore and demonstrated that global communications need never again be dependent on the available means of transport. Information moved to and from news agencies via the wireless (a mostly twentieth-century medium), transoceanic cables (widely established in the third quarter of the nineteenth century), and the overland telegraph (a mid-nineteenth century innovation). In terms of news dissemination, the *Titanic* disaster can be seen as the beginning of what the media guru Marshall McLuhan called the "Global Village," though he coined the term with 1960s satellite communication in mind.

Nowhere was the extent of this new telegraphic communications network more evident than in the news reports that reached the country farthest away from where the sinking occurred, Australia. Being so far away from the source of the story, Australian press coverage was limited to major updates, accompanied by an occasional cautious interpretation. It lacked the rampant speculation that characterized the North American news media.

Perhaps the "tyranny of distance," as they say down under, was, in this instance a blessing. And what a distance late-breaking information about the *Titanic* had to travel: early wireless reports reaching North America were relayed to England via cable; then eastward across Europe, the Middle East, and Asia, using overland and submarine lines; and, after arriving at Darwin in the north of Australia, the dispatches went south along the great overland telegraph to Adelaide and thence to major centers east and west.

Newspapers in other countries used some of the same means to access what at the time was called the "story of the century." Nevertheless, most of the information that went global arrived first in New York, where it was presented and interpreted by the most innovative assemblage of newspapers that graced any city. New York press coverage of the sinking attracted worldwide attention, and ultimately resulted in journalistic accomplishment being added to the city's list of internationally renowned achievements.

7

The Battle for New York

New York in 1912, diverse, lively, and not without its dangers, was the emerging metropolis of the new century. The *Titanic*'s planned maiden voyage from Great Britain to that city can be symbolically construed, along with countless other events at the time, as symptomatic of an inexorable passing of the torch of industrial and cultural leadership to New York from London, the urban monarch of the previous hundred years.

A less symbolic and more concrete indicator of the shift resides in the fact that the *Titanic*, pride of British mercantile shipping, was ultimately owned by a trust headed by New York's, America's, and the world's reigning doyen of dollars, J.P. Morgan. From his Fifth Avenue mansion he controlled a plethora of industries. Aging and too ill to occupy his personal suite on the *Titanic*, Morgan's physical demise followed the legendary ship's by a year; 1913 would also see the power of trusts such as his challenged by new federal legislation.

Another domain in which New York exerted leadership was journalism. As the terminus to which nearly all information roads led regarding the plight of the *Titanic*, no city had as many news-gathering resources. At least a dozen of the city's dailies took up the challenge of chasing the story. This tradition of a comprehensive popular press had been over three quarters of a century in the making. Its starting point can be traced to the birth of the *New York Sun* in 1833.

Founded by Benjamin Day and reinvigorated by Charles Dana in 1868, the *Sun* was the first of the "penny papers." This epithet referred not just to price but also to a new, implied, journalistic philosophy. Social issues, crime, scandal, and human-interest stories, along with sports and entertainment, were given regular extended coverage. As in the past, politics often guided editorial policy, but the views expressed now tended to be issue oriented rather than along party lines. They frequently anticipated the populist position that would make the papers of Joseph Pulitzer and William Randolph Hearst so successful by century's end.

The penny press also featured more rapid reportage of news than its predecessors. Born in an age when the railway and steamship made communication as well as transportation faster, the new journalism's addiction to rapid information movement was further fueled by the advent of the telegraph. During the 1840s this medium achieved a definitive separation of communication from transportation and ushered in the electric age; by the late 1860s the transatlantic cable enabled London news to appear in New York papers the next day.

Following on the heels of Day's successful venture with the *Sun* came James Gordon Bennett's *New York Herald* in 1835, and Horace "Go west, young man" Greeley's *New York Tribune* in 1841. This first wave of the penny press would be eventually challenged by the more sedate and information-oriented *New York Times*, founded in 1851 by Henry Raymond.

Reporting the story of the *Titanic* would involve all three representatives of the original penny press and a *Times* that had been reborn in 1896 when Adolph Ochs took over. It would also pose a major journalistic challenge for the two papers that actually led the city in circulation in 1912, Pulitzer's *New York World* and Hearst's *New York Journal*.

Pulitzer, a Hungarian immigrant, took over the *World* in 1883 after having performed a minor miracle the previous decade by reviving the ailing *St. Louis Post-Dispatch*. He increased the *World's* human-interest stories and conjured publicity stunts to boost circulation, such as sending Nellie Bly on a record-breaking 72-day trip around the world in 1888–89. The paper also outdid its competitors in the use of illustrations while maintaining quality editorials and adopting a distinctly populist and often pro-union position. By the mid-eighties the *World* had pulled even with the leading *Sun* and *Herald*. On the eve of the nineties, it became the paper of choice for the majority of New Yorkers.

A serious rival to the *World's* supremacy emerged in 1895, when Hearst took over the marginal *New York Journal*. Originally founded in 1882 as the *New York Morning Journal*, the paper was the brainchild, ironically enough, of Pulitzer's brother, Albert. The battle between Pulitzer and Hearst yielded yellow journalism, with Hearst taking some of the conventions of this tradition—scandal mongering, screaming headlines, and support for the underdog—to often ludicrous extremes.

Hearst also gained a reputation for news making when news reporting would not suffice. His most notorious foray in this direction occurred in 1898, when he drummed up sentiment for the United States to initiate the Spanish-American War. This episode, along with his famous quip to a reporter, "I'll furnish the war, you furnish the pictures," is humorously depicted in the first part of Orson Welles's cinematic masterpiece, *Citizen Kane*. The film goes on to elaborate several aspects of the rivalry between the *Journal* (called the *New York Inquirer*) and the *World* (dubbed the *New York Chronicle*). As we shall see, when confronted with having to cover the enormously difficult and important story of the *Titanic* in head-to-head competition with other New York dailies, Hearst's paper yielded a coverage that was nothing short of a journalistic disaster.

MONDAY, 15 APRIL

On this day in 1912, the world learned of the plight of the *Titanic*. Eerily, New York press coverage of the story can be seen as having commenced the previous day. The Sunday edition of the *Times* ran an article on page 6 describing the massiveness of the new ship and included a small photograph, which would wind up enlarged and moved to the front page the next day. Thus, from the outset, as well as throughout the coming weeks, the *Times* managed to be one step ahead of its rivals.

The first wireless reports stating the *Titanic* had struck an iceberg, was sinking by the bow, and putting women into lifeboats, reached newsrooms in the early morning hours of 15 April. Available information also indicated that several ships were rapidly steaming to her aid. Around these "facts," and a number of additional sketchy and sometimes conflicting messages, stories had to be written. With so few details, interpretation necessarily augmented reporting. That these interpretations varied considerably was due to the question marks surrounding the information. How fatal was the *Titanic*'s wound? Would she sink rapidly, slowly, or merely remain incapacitated at the surface? How quickly would potential rescue ships arrive, which even cautious papers such as the *Tribune* implied constituted a veritable armada.

The varying responses to these questions must have caused considerable consternation among readers perusing the newsstands. The tenor of the coverage ranged from the *Times*'s somber assemblage of evidence suggesting the worst to the imprudently optimistic exhortations of the *Journal*.

The *Times* account listed the known facts in an extended headline: "NEW LINER TITANIC HITS ICEBERG; SINKING BY THE BOW AT MIDNIGHT; WOMEN PUT OFF IN LIFE BOATS; LAST WIRELESS AT

12:27 A.M. BLURRED." The ominous follow-up text noted how the wireless transmissions ended abruptly and that the *Virginian* and *Baltic* were attempting to go to the *Titanic*'s position. It also mentioned the near miss the *Titanic* had with the liner *New York* when leaving Southampton and cited the *Niagara*'s earlier mishap with ice as evidence of the attendant dangers in the North Atlantic at that time of year. No other paper seemed to offer so little hope that all would be well.

The reserved *Tribune* ran most of the same information on its front page, but emphasized the "reassuring feature" that considerable assistance was on the way. The *Herald* did likewise, with part of its headline reading "VESSELS RUSH TO HER SIDE." Although we might easily take such a phrase for granted, for a 1912 readership attuned to every word, it implied that a concerted rescue effort had been deployed. The *Herald* added another glimmer of hope by running an article on the front page below its *Titanic* commentary that mentioned how the *Niagara* had hit ice in the same region as the *Titanic* and was nonetheless able to make her way to port.

The *Niagara* incident was elaborated upon at greater length in Pulitzer's *World*, where it served to temper a dire lead article that paralleled the *Times*'s assessment. The paper noted the *Niagara* was punctured twice by ice, and, although she summoned help, would-be rescuers were eventually waved off. For readers who were clinging to hope, the connotations must have been obvious: if the puny *Niagara* could survive such an encounter, why not the mighty *Titanic*?

The hint of hope became a virtual promise in the *Sun* and *Journal*. Although the morning *Sun* merely reported that the *Titanic* had hit an iceberg, the headline of the evening edition read, "TITANIC'S PASSENGERS ARE TRANSHIPPED." The subheadline claimed a rescue by the *Carpathia* and *Parisian*, with the *Titanic* being towed to Halifax by the *Virginian*. The headline of the final edition stated, "ALL SAVED FROM TITANIC AFTER COLLISION."

The accompanying article attributed this information to Captain Haddock of the *Olympic*. He later denied making any such statement. It probably resulted from wireless misinterpretation, whereby a transmission noting that the *Parisian* and *Carpathia* were headed to the site of the collision was construed as affirmation of an immediate rescue, with the information somehow linked to the *Olympic*'s captain. The *Sun*'s copywriters embellished the false story with their own description of the *Titanic*, still afloat with pumps laboring while her lifeboats were being rowed to the *Carpathia*. A contributing element to the elaboration of the scenario could have been the widely known and cited fact that the weather at the scene of the mishap was exceptionally calm and clear.

Hearst's *Journal*, using the boldest headline of any paper, was even more optimistic: "ALL SAFE ON TITANIC." A box to the left contained a subheadline claiming the liner was in tow, along with a picture of the ship and her captain. Subsequent commentary posited that four vessels were involved in the rescue, which was facilitated by calm seas. More specific pronouncements soon followed. One statement had twenty lifeboats (which, probably unbeknownst to the paper, was the *Titanic's* full complement) going to the *Carpathia*. Later it was noted that survivors were also picked up by the *Baltic* and *Virginian,* and that a wireless message stated that there were no casualties. Sources are not cited for any of this information. One suspects the paper's penchant for creating reader-friendly copy when information was not forthcoming. This occurred overtly on page 2, when the alleged towing of the *Titanic* by the *Virginian* was described in the manner in which it might have taken place.

Several papers outside New York also elected to print the "all safe, *Titanic* in tow" story in their 15 April editions, despite the sketchiness of the information. They included the *Springfield Evening Union*, the *Columbus Evening Dispatch*, and the *Montreal Star*. Although some of this false information was routed via Montreal, that city's other English language daily, the *Gazette,* did not go with the rescue story. In deciding to run it, the rival *Star* put out three extras. The first described the ship still afloat; the second cited White Star's reassurance that she was safe; however, by the third edition the increasing uncertainty of the story yielded the headline, "SS TITANIC IN BAD SHAPE." Montreal's weekly paper, the *Witness,* which came out on 16 April, refused to abandon the hopeful news, and ran the story a day after most other sources had conceded the ship was lost.

When more and verifiable information regarding the *Titanic's* plight came into New York newsrooms later on the 15th, it made the next day's edition of each paper pivotal. The cautiously pessimistic *Times* gained public confidence, while the *Sun* and *Journal* struggled to maintain a readership they had earlier misled.

TUESDAY, 16 APRIL

Building on its previous guesstimate of the disaster's magnitude, the *Times* ran a headline that put the death toll at 1,250, with 866 assumed survivors. Among those saved, the paper listed as definite the Director of White Star and President of International Mercantile Marine, Bruce Ismay, and as a maybe, the young Mrs. Astor. Subsequent front-page commentary served to remind readers of the paper's prescience of the day before, noting that White Star did not concede the liner was lost until 8:20 the previous evening and that the widely circulated reports about the *Titanic* having been towed by the *Virginian* had no foundation. A large photograph (normally not the *Times* style) of the ship being towed out of Belfast, perhaps for her trials, accompanied the headline. Page 2 contained another photograph of the ship along with a detailed map of where the sinking took place, with the position of nearby ships also shown.

Although the *Times*'s coverage would become widely lauded, it was not without contradictions and speculation. One of the articles noted that there were only 655 survivors, a deviation from the headline. The piece also assumed there were too few lifeboats to accommodate all the passengers on board. This required a bit of deduction, since the White Star office in New York claimed not to have that information.

The person in charge there was Phillip Franklin, Vice President and General Manager of International Mercantile Marine. It was Franklin who, for almost a full day after the first reports of trouble, insistently denied that the ship had foundered. He would later be accused of knowing the worst while refusing to acknowledge it publicly. Perhaps no one was as chastised during this stage of the reporting, especially by papers who ran stories consistent with his denials. Fortunately for him, public animosity eventually went up the chain of command and was transferred to his boss, Bruce Ismay, soon after the *Carpathia* docked on the evening of 18 April.

Did Franklin really not know how many lifeboats the *Titanic* carried? If so, the *Times* did not make an issue of it. Their research had already uncovered the number on her sister ship, the *Olympic*: sixteen plus four collapsibles, yielding space for 1,180 persons. Readers were left to ponder the unlikely possibility that the *Titanic* had carried more.

Confident that the important and decisive features of the disaster were now established with certainty, the 16 April *Times* then engaged in a speculative filling in of details. Several paragraphs described the rescue, while others focused on the circumstances of the collision. This strategy was acknowledged by using the words "must have" to describe the alleged events. The paper also suggested that the shock of the impact perhaps destroyed the operation of the electrically operated watertight doors (not the case), and that the iceberg could have opened gaps further along the hull (an accurate guess). In support of its assessment of the possible collision scenario, the paper mentioned the *Olympic*'s encounter with the *Hawke* as an indicator of the poor maneuverability and vulnerability of the new generation of giant liners. Several maritime experts were interviewed who supported these contentions, and they in turn added insights pertaining to the dangers of ice in the North Atlantic at that time of year.

The remainder of the coverage monitored reactions around the world, as well as in different parts of New York. It also presented a gallery of some of the notable passengers on the voyage, gave a summary of Captain Smith's career, and provided an annotated list of previous maritime disasters. In all, there were eight pages of meticulous, well-organized copy, setting a standard for other papers to match. None could.

The *Tribune* estimated that there were 1,340 casualties and 866 survivors, most of the latter being women and children. What no one at the time could have realized was that, given the presence of crewmen in many of the lifeboats, one-third of the survivors would turn out to be men. Covering some of the same ground as the *Times* but with less detail, the *Tribune* also discussed the new giant liners, the dangers of ice, and the career of Captain Smith. As befitted its business orientation, the paper contained an article on the probable insurance loss entailed by the disaster.

The *Herald,* which in reporting the disaster on 15 April had broken with its regular format of putting classified ads on the front page, now went to an even greater extreme. A bold slanted headline announced that the ship had sunk with 1,800 on board and that there were 675 survivors. It was accompanied by a spectacular drawing of the collision, creating the most eye-catching front-page report of the tragedy that my research unearthed. Whoever did the artwork is uncredited—to cite the person would of course detract from the realism implied in the illustration—but the style is evident in other issues of the paper throughout that week.

In going over ground also covered by the *Times* and *Tribune,* the *Herald* included more commentary on the false reports of rescue, noting in a subheadline that after the collision the "WHOLE WORLD THOUGHT TITANIC SAFE." Whoever wrote this seemed not to have had in mind devoted *Times* readers.

The headline of the *World* listed 1,500 lost (the most accurate estimate) and 866 survivors. Consistent with the paper's tradition of exposé journalism, it made White Star's early denial of the sinking into a topic for critical commentary. Without accusing Phillip Franklin of deceit, his professed ignorance of the number of lifeboats on the *Titanic* was implied to be the next worst thing, along with the reassurances he gave that the ship's unsinkable status would enable her to float after any collision with ice. With only five pages of coverage in its 16 April issue, the *World* might have felt that it had said all that had to be said. However, the paper may have either lacked the resources to handle the story more fully or simply felt more coverage was unnecessary.

The papers that had the most difficult decision regarding what to print on 16 April were the *Sun* and *Journal.* The previous day both had elected to go with stories of complete rescue. Now, knowing the worst, they had to soft-pedal it to save face.

The morning edition of the *Sun*, rather than conceding that 1,500 were lost, used the phrase "1500 MISSING" in its headline. The ice thus broken, to use an unforgivable pun, the evening edition could then state that 1,400 perished, 800 were saved, and that only one ship, the *Carpathia*, was involved in the rescue; however, the final edition did hint that the *Virginian* might have more survivors. Blame for the earlier false reports was implied to reside with White Star. This was accomplished through chronicling the pandemonium that surrounded their New York office and the inaccurate information the company released. What the paper failed to note was that White Star only issued denials of the worst, not details on how the alleged rescue and towing took place. Responsibility for this information resided with those newspapers that reported it on the basis of meager evidence. Having thus attempted to make peace with its readers, the *Sun* settled down to the business of discussing what was known about the sinking, the conditions surrounding it, and personalities involved.

How did Hearst's *Journal* face its readers on the 16th? With a modicum of deceit. The same screaming headlines that had announced "ALL SAFE" the previous day, now declared "866 SAVED," with *"VIRGINIAN* TOO LATE" just below in muted gray characters one-quarter the size. For the paper to preface the initial headline with "only" would have been a concession to journalistic honesty it was not prepared to make. How many people actually perished? To find the estimates, *Journal* readers had to consult the text of subsequent pages.

To further encourage amnesia among its subscribers regarding the previous issue, the paper raised the question of initial culpability for the loss of life. White Star was targeted. Several articles, including the editorial, dealt with the "titanic crime" of the ship not having an adequate complement of lifeboats. Other pieces, amply illustrated, stressed the dangers of ice in North Atlantic shipping routes.

Another kind of danger suggested in the *Journal*'s coverage—to the eye of some moralistic beholders—was of the lovely young Madeleine Astor. Several siren-like portraits of her appeared, along with a statement announcing that her husband's body had just been found close to the site where the ship went down. Astor's divorce and eventual marriage to this nineteen year old just before the voyage had created an international scandal. The *Journal*'s reaction to the liaison was more along the lines of celebrity watching than moralizing. (Hearst himself would later raise eyebrows by having an extended affair with the young actress Marion Davies.)

WEDNESDAY, 17 APRIL

As anxious readers sought their paper of choice, few held out any hope that the tragedy would be of a lesser magnitude than reported the previous day. What they did hope for were more details and a possible explanation for why, on the clearest of evenings, an experienced captain commanding a state-of-the-art ship allowed it to collide with an iceberg and founder. For anyone following the story it was obvious from earlier coverage, as well as expert testimony, that the collision could not have been the iceberg's fault; in other words, it was in the region it was supposed to be in, given the time of year and earlier navigational reports. Why, then, was the *Titanic*, whose role was that of a speeding interloper into a known colony of natural hazards, so rudely oblivious to the residents?

Answers could only be hinted at, and carefully at best. Without doubt, most papers were conscious of the possible embarrassment of reporting something that would later turn out to be otherwise—most papers, that is, except Hearst's *Journal*, which took one more stab at chronicling an important turn of events overlooked by rivals. As we shall see, the result was another news-guessing error that further diminished the paper's credibility. In following a more cautious strategy, the rest of the New York press corps subordinated conclusive statements about what happened to an elaboration of the context surrounding the voyage and sinking. Archival sources and expert commentary aided the task.

Once again, the *Times* took the lead in providing detailed comprehensive coverage. Its efforts the previous two days had probably succeeded in attracting readers who normally subscribed to rival papers. Circulation figures suggest this, for although the number of copies sold for all papers increased, it was most pronounced in the case of the *Times*.

What was known with certainty was the passenger manifest, which the *Times* printed. Readers could then compare it to a subsequent list containing the names of 400 known survivors, which had come in via the *Carpathia's* meager wireless reports. What made many of the names that appeared on the first list but not the second so interesting was their social status. Reliable reports already put John Jacob Astor among the deceased, which led to an awareness that wealth and privilege had provided no insurance against the consequences of this nautical Armageddon. When other famous names did not appear on initial survivor lists, or were noted as missing, their possible demise piqued the interest of many.

The *Times's* response to this fascination with the rich and famous was to devote most of the 17 April front page to photographs, drawings, and biographical profiles of some of the notables who had made the nightmare voyage. In a number of instances, their understandably distraught family members provided statements.

By page 3, technical and regulatory details earned consideration. The features of the ship were described, along with reactions to the disaster voiced by authorities in London, most notably Lloyd's, who faced a phenomenal insurance loss. The paper's investigation of Lloyd's role in the tragedy was one of the few areas in which it had not been first, since the *Tribune* had already broached the issue a day earlier. What the *Times* added was a citation of the British Board of Trade regulations governing the number of lifeboats on a ship: that vessels of 10,000 tons or more must carry a minimum of sixteen boats. The *Titanic*, almost five times that tonnage, carried twenty—wholly inadequate, but more than the rules stipulated. The paper then joined the growing chorus demanding the rule be changed. In doing likewise, the rival *Herald* noted that United States regulations required lifeboats for all on board. Nevertheless, we must remember that the country was not endowed with Olympic class liners capable of carrying 3,000-plus passengers; a full complement of lifeboats would limit valuable deck space, or so Bruce Ismay and White Star had earlier decided.

In subsequent pages, the *Times* discussed again the dangers of ice. There were photographs of icebergs, and one of the crushed bow of the *Arizona* taken after her spectacular but benign collision with such a hazard in 1879. This line of inquiry included an article on the *Niagara*, along with a statement by Captain Inman Selby of the *Republic* that echoed the previous day's speculation that the *Titanic's* collision was probably along the lines of a glancing blow that sliced open a considerable portion of the ship's hull. The day's coverage concluded with a chart of the ocean depth where the sinking took place and a final query as to whether such massive and luxurious vessels are desirable.

One final point should be noted with respect to the 17 April *Times*. The paper could not resist suggesting to readers that its coverage was widely regarded as the most complete and up-to-date. Page 5 contained a self-congratulatory article describing how crowds were being attracted to the *New York Times* building by the regularly posted bulletins, which in turn were being sent "far and wide" to places such as hotels and Pennsylvania Station.

The *Tribune* devoted the bulk of its commentary, as did many papers, to the notables who might have gone down with the ship. The *Herald*, using the work of the unnamed illustrator mentioned previously, went with a headline story that claimed the ship was "torn asunder" while traveling at 18 knots. At the time this may have seemed to readers to be an impressive and reckless speed, but the actual rate surpassed the conjecture. At the American inquiry it would be later learned that something in the vicinity of 22 knots was the actual speed—not quite the maximum 24 knots of which she might have been capable, but close.

The *Herald*'s coverage exceeded the *Tribune*'s in length and was only slightly less than that of the *Times*. Going over some of the same ground as the latter, the *Arizona* incident was discussed and illustrated with a drawing (the *Times* used a photograph) of her wrecked bow. Comparative interest in the two collisions was then piqued by an eyewitness description from an *Arizona* passenger who had observed events thirty-two years earlier. Speculation on how the *Titanic*'s damage may have differed was offered by a naval architect, W.A. Dobson. He accurately proposed that the *Titanic* may have tried to avoid hitting the iceberg and in so doing sideswiped it, resulting in a gash along the hull for most of the ship's length. The paper ended its coverage by proposing the establishment of a government patrol to warn of ice, an idea that eventually came to pass with the formation of the International Ice Patrol.

Speculation about the nature of the collision, along with comments on the physical features of the ship and an updated survivor list, can also be found in the 17 April edition of the *World*. Consistent with the celebrity watching no paper was immune from, the coverage included an article on Vincent Astor. Now aware of his father's death, he was described as being in the throes of preparing to send for the recovered body. The issue of who died and why was further elaborated in a discussion of the wisdom and history of the edict, "Women and children first." In the coming weeks it would emerge as a source for debate in many quarters.

Still retreating from its overly optimistic headline two days earlier, the 17 April *Sun*'s coverage was surprisingly cautious and brief. However, one area that received extended commentary, given the paper's business orientation, was an assessment of the financial wherewithal aboard the ship and the ensuing loss.

Unlike the *Sun*, the *Journal* failed to heed the earlier lesson about not proclaiming sketchy information to be unequivocal fact. The 17 April headline blared, "EVERY WOMAN SAVED." The paper's reasons for this pronouncement will forever remain a mystery. The headline must have been just as much an affront to common sense then as now. How could a chaotic accident at sea, which claimed approximately 1,500 lives (clearly established by 17 April), with an estimated 600-800 survivors, not result in the loss of life of at least a few women? Despite the call for women and children first, the ship's condition and the ensuing evacuation posed obvious hazards for anyone attempting to leave.

We should also wonder why Hearst reporters, who were attending David Sarnoff in the wireless room of Wanamaker's Department Store, did not pick up on the fact that the names of survivors coming in included a disproportionately high number of men, especially given the way the evacuation was *supposed* to have taken place. Perhaps editors were bedazzled into thinking that the fate of Madeleine Astor, who appeared in yet another large and this time ravishing portrait, was representative of all women on board.

THURSDAY, 18 APRIL

What every paper reported was that the *Carpathia* would be landing in New York by early evening. The names of those who survived, as well as the casualties, would then be known with cold certainty. Most readers were also expecting the ship's arrival to clear up the mystery of how and why the sinking occurred. Alas, the initial answers would only raise more questions. It would take the better part of another week for the American inquiry to present a convincing case regarding what had happened.

One fact of which New York newspapers *were* certain on 18 April was that with the arrival of the *Carpathia* they would not be the only press corps having access to eyewitness testimony regarding the disaster. Reporters from many parts of North America were descending on the city for what promised to be the most massive journalistic scramble in history.

The *Times* was well prepared for the challenge; so were New York's municipal authorities. The paper noted pertinent information relating to the expected event and queried the *Carpathia*'s frustratingly minimal communications over the previous three days. The issue of the false reports of complete rescue was again addressed and, in conjunction with a note about the forthcoming inquiry, led to a call for greater wireless regulation. Needless to say, there was also much recapitulation of information the paper ran earlier that week. The coverage concluded by suggesting that the next day's edition would mark a turning point in our knowledge of the tragedy.

The *Tribune* also re-presented some of its earlier coverage, but included an updated article in which Phillip Franklin was allowed to present his case that White Star did not withhold vital information from the public. The *Herald* mentioned the Senate Inquiry and went on to note the one to be convened in London at a later unspecified date. Consistent with the exciting visuals it had been presenting throughout the week was a front-page illustration of the *Titanic* going down with lifeboats beside her and the iceberg in the background. Page 3 included a photograph of an iceberg with a cleverly drawn-in likeness of the *Titanic* behind it.

Going over previous coverage was also a strategy the *World* employed. The paper marshalled available evidence to present a summary account of what might have happened, knowing that the next day it would be measured against the words of those who were there. That these words would often be contradictory probably helped soften later criticism directed at the interpretive license taken by the press as a whole. One final point worth noting regarding the *World*'s coverage is that in each day's paper they presented a news cartoon critically commenting on some aspect of the disaster. This practice was widespread, but in my opinion the *World* did it with more poignancy than any other paper I have surveyed, American or otherwise.

The *Sun*, after having gradually recovered credibility from its inaccurately optimistic headline of the 15th, used the edition of the 18th to summarize events to date. One area it amplified, which had only been mentioned by rival papers, was the preparations being made for the survivors. Several articles were given over to describing the lodging and support that would be provided. In most instances, the individuals and groups responsible were mentioned by name.

Not surprisingly, the strangest lead story of the day came from the *Journal*. On the basis of what must have been meager evidence—probably several wireless reports from survivors—the paper discussed how a number of them had been rendered ill by their ordeal. The remainder of the coverage dealt with reaction to the disaster, the known facts pertaining to it, and the upcoming inquiry. However, one area where the paper did something unique and interesting had to do with events slated to transpire that evening. On page 3 there was a large photograph of pier 54, where the *Carpathia* would land, and an explanation of how the passengers would probably disembark.

The *Carpathia*'s arrival would initiate a new dimension in reporting what was already being called "the story of the century." So far, the press battle for New York had not resulted in a decisive victory for any of the participants, although the *Times* had perhaps surprised many by taking the initial lead; today, it is the first paper mentioned when *Titanic* aficionados discuss press responses to the tragedy. Their reactions are usually influenced by the 19 April edition. It gained worldwide attention and bestowed a prominence to the paper during the coming week that no rival could match.

Nevertheless, honorable mention for coverage during those crucial first four days should go to the *Herald*. The paper used exciting visuals and thoughtful articles to cover a salient range of topics. At the other end of the press continuum, it might be appropriate to award a booby prize to Hearst's *Journal* for its misguided sensationalism.

8

Carr Van Anda and the *New York Times*

The successes in the battle for New York that the *Times* attained with its coverage attracted worldwide notoriety. Fourteen years earlier, when Adolph Ochs took over the paper, the circulation was 9,000 and dropping; out of fifteen dailies in the city, the *Times* stood thirteenth.

To the rest of the world the *Times*'s rise following the disaster may have given the appearance of a sudden transition from obscurity to prominence, but it had been over a decade in the making. During those years three elements converged, and any assessment of the *Times*'s *Titanic* coverage should acknowledge them: the papers historical commitment to leading-edge investigative reporting; Ochs's plan to extend this mandate in a more efficient and comprehensive manner; and the innovative field generalship of managing editor Carr Van Anda, who was hired in 1904.

The paper first came into existence on 18 September 1851 as the *New-York Daily Times*—the word "daily" was dropped in 1857, and the hyphen in 1896. It was founded by Henry Raymond, whose name would be eventually added to a pantheon of nineteenth-century American press pioneers that includes Benjamin Day of the *New York Sun,* James Gordon Bennett of the *New York Herald,* and Horace Greeley of the *New York Tribune.* The *Times*'s early commitment to rapid news gathering, rather than extensive editorializing, was demonstrated in its coverage of the Civil War. In those early years Raymond also deemed that news is a phenomenon that includes what goes on in the literary and cultural worlds. To that end, a Sunday edition was launched in 1861. One of Ochs's first decisions when taking over in 1896 was to revamp and expand it, thereby creating a ritual for people that still thrives.

Up until 1884, the *Times* was Republican in affiliation—"the party of Lincoln," as it was often called by supporters—but the paper maintained an independence that was not pleasing to party extremists. With Raymond's death in 1869, his trusted lieutenant, George Jones, took over. He led the *Times* into the 1870s with one of the major American news stories of the century: the exposure of Boss Tweed and his ring of New York municipal corruption.

The 1880s saw the rise of Joseph Pulitzer's *New York World.* Increased sensationalism also began to typify several metropolitan dailies. It would lead to the yellow journalism of the '90s, when William Randolph Hearst took over the *New York Journal.* The *Times's* leadership was uncertain as to how to respond and circulation declined. The beginning of the paper's slide, however, was marked by a spectacular scoop, the last one under the regime of Jones, who would die in 1891. The story involved a mishap at sea and prefigured the paper's coverage of events in 1912.

On Sunday, 14 May 1886 (same day and day of the month as the *Titanic* disaster), a rumor circulated the waterfront that the Cunarder *Oregon* had been involved in a collision off Fire Island, and that most or all of the 1,000 on board had been picked up by the German liner *Fulda.* City editor William J. Kenny gathered his staff, much as Carr Van Anda would a generation later, and got down to maritime basics. From tide tables and ship data they knew that the *Fulda* could not cross Sandy Hook before high tide at midnight, therefore it would be 3 A.M. before she reached quarantine, where boarding and information gathering could be effected. This would preclude coverage of the story in Monday's edition.

According to Meyer Berger in his partisan history of the *Times,* Kenny and staff then braved a severe storm to charter a tugboat to take them to the *Fulda.* The agreement with the tug's captain, who was understandably hesitant to leave port given the conditions, called for the newspapermen to double as crew. En route they encountered a smaller tug in distress and took her in tow, only to find out that one of her passengers was a *New York Sun* reporter. Kenny persuaded the captain not to allow the reporter on board, and, after safely depositing the smaller vessel in a quiet cove, the larger one continued on her mission.

Under the pretext of being health officers, the *Times's* men boarded the *Fulda.* When her captain discovered the ruse, a melée ensued. The *Times* men scattered, found the *Oregon's* master with some of the survivors, and gleaned the story of the shipwreck and miraculous survival of all involved. Wrapping their notes around heavy cutlery, Kenny and his press commandos then bolted for the top deck. Another confrontation arose. One reporter made a spectacular leap to the waiting tug; the others threw all the weighted copy onto her deck before being arrested. The 15 May edition recounted the complete saga of the *Oregon* while not a word of it appeared in rival papers.

The *Times's* astute coverage of maritime incidents would be demonstrated again in 1908 with an exclusive account of the *Cymric's* rescue of most of the *St. Cuthbert's* crew. Ditto in 1909, with the paper's detailed account of how Jack Binns's wireless heroics enabled the *Baltic* to rescue those on board the *Republic* and *Florida* following their collision (both incidents are discussed in chapter 3). By 1912 no paper had a better track record covering maritime mishaps, and none was more prepared to handle the kind of scenario that involved the *Titanic*.

Unfortunately, in the years leading up to 1896, the *Times* itself had become a sinking vessel. New leadership seemed the only possible rescue. It came from an unlikely source in the person of Adolph Ochs. He was a southerner with a background as a printer rather than as a news writer, but he had been modestly successful in guiding the *Chattanooga Times* to solvency. Born of German-Jewish parents in 1858, Ochs had an entrepreneurial spirit tempered by a willingness to proceed cautiously and meticulously toward his goals. In taking over the *New York Times*, he sought to return the paper to the spirit of Henry Raymond—minus the Republican Party politics—although critics of his early years at the helm accused the paper of favoring big business.

On 19 August 1896, a reborn *Times* hit the street bearing Ochs's declaration of principles. The famous slogan, "All the News That's Fit to Print," made its first appearance on the masthead on 10 February 1897. The maxim was the work of the paper's staff and just as contentious then as now, with its suggestion of a kind of censorship. A contest was held to find a better phrase. A winner was chosen and duly awarded the $100 prize for "All the World's News, but not a School for Scandal." Wisely, the staff decided their original effort was superior and retained it.

Ochs streamlined and expanded the paper. He also tried various new ways to attract subscribers, such as telephone solicitation. Circulation increased, as did the esteem of the paper. Then, in 1904, Ochs made a decision that would give the *Times* national and ultimately international stature: he hired Carr Van Anda as managing editor.

Van Anda, a.k.a. "V.A." or "Boss" in the news room, was born in 1864 in Georgetown, Ohio, and came to the *Times* after sixteen years on the rival *Sun*. Histories of American journalism describe him as one of the most eminent managing editors to ever work an American daily. A supreme tactician of news gathering, he also had an exceptional knowledge of science and history. Two incidents dramatized to colleagues his knowledge in the latter areas: the discovery of a mistake in the translation of a paper by Einstein, which duly impressed the great scientist; and the time Van Anda's ability to read Egyptian hieroglyphics led him to spot inaccuracies in a genealogy of Tut-Ankh-Amen, which the British Museum promptly corrected. He was also a gifted lecturer and excellent writer on a variety of topics, but he rarely allowed his name to appear in conjunction with something he had written, nor did he grant interviews.

Ochs, in contrast, was neither an intellectual nor a practicing journalist. Nevertheless, his vision of what the *Times* could and should be powerfully complemented Van Anda's sense of strategy and detail, thereby creating an extraordinary partnership.

Much of the promise of the new century the *Times* was entering derived from applied scientific research leading to improvements in transportation and communication. Perusal of the paper from 1904 to 1912 reveals numerous articles on these topics, many commissioned and some written by Van Anda.

In 1907 it was Van Anda who proposed a transatlantic news service using wireless. Marconi doubted that all the elements needed were sufficiently developed. The *Times's* editor convinced him otherwise and took the initiative in organizing the setup. The transmission sequence began in London, with information traveling by telegraph to Clifton, where it would be held until noon (7 A.M. Eastern Standard Time), then sent by wireless to Glace Bay, Nova Scotia. From there it would go via telegraph to New York, Van Anda having arranged to lease the Glace Bay–New York line each day at the same time. The plan met opposition and skepticism, but it worked. The total cost was half of what would have had to be paid if the transatlantic cable were used to convey the same messages. Over the years Van Anda expanded the network and, in 1919, had a wireless station set up in the *Times* building.

In the years leading up to the *Titanic* tragedy, Van Anda helped coordinate coverage of a series of major stories that helped raise the fortunes of the paper: the Russian-Japanese War in 1904–1905; Peary reaching the North Pole in 1909 (a *Times* exclusive); and the Jim Jeffries–Jack Johnson heavyweight championship fight in 1910 (with commentary to the *Times* provided by former champion John L. Sullivan). As impressive as these accomplishments were, they would pale in comparison to coverage of the chain of events that began shortly before midnight 14 April 1912.

According to *Times* historian, Meyer Berger, in the early morning hours of the 15th Van Anda was talking to the telegraph editor when a dispatch came through stating the *Titanic* had struck an iceberg and was sending out a CQD for assistance. Just as his precursor William J. Kenny did in 1886 when information came in about the *Oregon,* Van Anda assembled his troops and drafted a campaign plan. He sent one man to the morgue (the paper's archives) to gather all known facts about the ship, another to search for information about who the passengers were, and a third to secure the last description of the *Titanic* and to find out about hazards in the North Atlantic at that time of year.

According to Van Anda's biographer Barnett Fine, activity in the news room at this time was intense but with no hint of panic, as the telegraph clicked, phones rang, and typewriters pounded. When no further information on the ship's plight came over the wire, Van Anda suspected the worst. With the press already rolling for the mail edition, he ordered the lead story to be replaced by the headline, "TITANIC SINKING IN MID-OCEAN; HIT GREAT ICEBERG." Several hours later the city edition also voiced a worst case scenario and supplemented the contention with information that had been gathered by the staff during those hectic early morning hours. During the excitement none of the staff had noticed that an advertisement for the return voyage appeared on page 11.

No other paper had as much coverage, and none seemed as convinced the ship was doomed. Van Anda had taken a great risk, but a well-informed one. Within twenty-four hours the magnitude of the tragedy was acknowledged by White Star's New York office; they had earlier denied the seriousness of the situation to Van Anda when he inquired by telephone. The *Times* earned national and international attention for its astute coverage, as well as through the sale of some of its stories to other papers over the next several days. But the saga of the disaster was far from over, and the *Times*'s campaign to cover it had only just begun.

With the *Carpathia* slated to arrive in New York Thursday night, 18 April, Van Anda booked a floor of the Strand Hotel at 11th Avenue and 14th Street, just a few hundred yards from where the ship would dock. He arranged for the suites to be connected directly to the *Times* office by telegraph and telephone. Since no reporters would be allowed on board the *Carpathia,* it seemed the paper would have to scramble for stories on a level playing field with its rivals. If this was to be the case, the initial assault would have to be well coordinated. Van Anda's lieutenant, day editor Arthur Greaves, sent sixteen reporters to the scene, although press passes to the pier were limited to only four per newspaper. He also plotted their itineraries and provided advice. Meanwhile, Van Anda worked out a plan that would give the *Times*'s coverage a decisive edge on all its rivals.

He sent reporter Jim Speers to Marconi, who at the time was dining with his New York manager, John Bottomley. Van Anda then contacted the inventor by telephone to persuade him to board the ship with Speers. Marconi indicated that he was indeed planning to board later that evening in order to talk to his two wireless men: Harold Bride, who had survived from the *Titanic,* and Harold Cottam of the *Carpathia.* Van Anda's sense of the urgency of the situation led Marconi and Bottomley to interrupt their dinner and head for the ship with Speers. Routes and transportation were suggested by Van Anda, who had worked out a strategy to enable the men to circumnavigate the growing congestion of people and vehicles.

Although things might have happened this way, the spontaneity suggested by the scenario seems odd given earlier wireless transmissions to the *Carpathia* sent by Marconi's chief engineer in New York, Frederick Sammis. The messages, which urged the Marconi operators on board to withhold information in anticipation of an arranged exclusive, arrived several hours before the ship docked on 18 April. They were intercepted by the Navy and brought to light by Senator Smith at the American Inquiry. Marconi's subsequent denial of knowledge regarding these dispatches has few believers among those who have assessed the incident, the present writer included.

As police barricades held back a throng of between 30,000 and 50,000 people, Marconi, Bottomley, and Speers made their way toward the ship at approximately 9:30 P.M. When stopped by police they pleaded their case. According to Berger, the status of all three was declared, whereupon the officer in question said something about no reporters being allowed on board and then, mistaking Bottomley for Speers, held him back and let the other two up the gangplank. One suspects that a more deliberate ruse might have been conjured, given the strong mandate police had to keep reporters off the ship.

Speers took down Bride's account as quickly as possible and then rushed back to the *Times* office to get his notes rendered into copy. The interview became the lead story on the front page of the morning edition. The rapidity with which this all transpired—the edition went to press at 12:30 A.M., 19 April—would be impressive even in the current era of electronic news gathering and typesetting.

The interview was somewhat stream of consciousness and contained several "facts" that would be changed, and in some cases absent, in Bride's testimony at the American Inquiry. Under the circumstances, some misquotation or misinterpretation on the part of Speers is understandable, and even the slight shift in Bride's recall of the sinking is not unusual for survivors of a chaotic and complex trauma.

Bride began by defending the limited wireless communication about the disaster that came from the *Carpathia.* He contended that he and Cottam had their hands full sending out messages pertaining to the survivors. He also claimed that the ship best able to receive their transmissions, the U.S. Navy's *Chester,* had "wretched operators" who were "as slow as Christmas coming," adding that although they knew American Morse code the Navy men were not well versed in its continental equivalent. Whether or not this was true, the emphasis Bride gave it indicates he probably felt his actions might be subject to later scrutiny, as indeed they were at the American inquiry. Rather than pursue Bride's points further, by ascertaining the competence of Navy operators, Senator Smith preferred to explore the issue of wireless practice by concentrating on Marconi.

Bride went on to recount the circumstances of that fatal night, noting how he barely felt the collision. Shortly after the *Titanic* hit the iceberg, Captain Smith showed up in the Marconi cabin and asked the two operators to send the regulation international call for help and to stand by. They sent the CQD. When Smith returned with the grave news, the Marconi men maintained their composure and sense of humor. Bride admitted suggesting that Phillips send the new SOS call, pointing out that another opportunity to do so might not occur. In a more somber vein, he also described the incident whereby he had to knock out the stoker trying to steal Phillips's lifebelt.

During the ship's last moments, Bride told of helping to disengage a collapsible lifeboat and then being washed overboard. While struggling in the freezing water, he kept hearing the band. Three times during the interview he mentioned the last tune played, "Autumn," although he did not indicate whether the piece was the Episcopal hymn or the popular song "Songe d'Automne." Little did anyone realize at the time how the question of what the band played would live on as an enduring aspect of the history of those terrifying final moments.

Subsequent events of that night were elaborated in stark detail. Bride described how he was pulled aboard the overturned collapsible then transferred to one of the partially filled lifeboats, where he noticed the body of Phillips; at the American Inquiry he would credit this observation to another, unnamed person. Plagued by injured legs throughout his sojourn on the *Carpathia*, Bride nonetheless told of his offer to assist Cottam in the Marconi cabin. And again, this time in conclusion, he restated the reasons for his retentive communication, decrying the *Chester's* operators a third time.

The article is riveting. Of all the eyewitness accounts to appear in the press, Bride's became the most cited. It established for posterity the courageous actions of Phillips. This must have pleased Marconi, for with Phillips not around to receive the accolades, some of them were directed his way. The public ceded more heroism to the inventor than was his due, even after Senator Smith's exposé of the collusion with Van Anda. Finally, Bride's "earwitness" account of the band playing until the bitter end added to a growing legend. However, at the time the public wanted the last song to be the more memorable one that less credible witnesses claimed they heard: "Nearer, My God To Thee." Popular culture, through films such as *Titanic* and *A Night to Remember*, has made it so.

At the time Speers was interviewing Bride, the *Carpathia's* Marconi man, Cottam, left the ship and headed for the *Times* office to add his observations to the accounts that would appear in the morning edition. That this was prearranged, as was the interview with Bride, seems likely; that both men were paid is established fact. Van Anda biographer Barnett Fine even has Cottam wandering by accident into the *New York Herald* building in his quest for the *Times* office; needless to say, Cottam recounted nothing until he reached his destination.

Neither Fine nor Berger nor Elmer Davies, in their historical assessments of the *Times*, question the ethics involved in gathering these stories. Senator Smith did, and his views were amplified by other newspapers, most notably those of Pulitzer and Hearst, which the above-mentioned *Times* chroniclers seem not to have consulted. The Cottam interview appeared on page 2, and it made the paper's coverage all the more impressive.

Around these two spectacular scoops, the *Times* deployed numerous observations and accounts gleaned from whomever their platoon of reporters could elicit commentary. The edition contained thirteen pages of coverage, with pages 12 and 13 given over to the names of those known to be missing.

It was an astounding feat of rapid news gathering. Understandably, the stories could not always be checked for accuracy, and the urgency to take down as much information as rapidly as possible led to some verbose and occasional silly statements. The paper's own copywriters were not immune to such lapses. Witness the following example taken from the front page article next to the Bride interview:

In a clear starlit night that showed a clear deep blue sea for miles and miles, the *Titanic,* an hour after she had struck a submerged iceberg at full speed and head on, sank slowly to her ocean grave.

With "clear" repeated twice, the use of the phrase "miles and miles," plus the length of the sentence, it would have a hard time passing muster in English 101 or the scrutiny of Joseph Pulitzer. Less forgivable in the above passage is the assumption that the ship struck the iceberg "head on." Perhaps the statement was written prior to the scramble for stories dockside, since comments that appear later in the paper refer to the ship as having only grazed the iceberg; almost everyone interviewed who was aware of the impact noted how minimal it was.

Getting the stories typeset as soon as they were available also created an order of priority that did not always reflect what we would now deem to be the importance of the information in question. For example, the two front-page articles on either side of Bride's story contained a series of statements that the *Times* conceded could in some instances be "hearsay" or "rumor." Then, tucked away in the middle of page 3, we find Lawrence Beesley's keen-eyed and thoughtfully worded account. He would go on to write a book about the disaster, which appeared later that year: *The Loss of SS Titanic: Its Story and Its Lessons.*

In the hearsay and rumor category, we find frequent commentary regarding the *Titanic's* most notorious survivor, Bruce Ismay, the managing director of the line. One interviewee claimed Ismay paid the crew of a lifeboat, another stated that a group of women in a partially filled boat beseeched him to enter. Ismay did not get his say until page 7. He denied the ship was either trying to set a record or traveling at full speed. When confronted with the issue of his survival, he claimed he got off on the last boat and then declined further questions. In a subsequent statement at the American inquiry, he said he boarded a lifeboat (not the last one) of his own volition since the boat was being lowered and there was nobody else in the vicinity.

Another popular source of speculation was Captain Smith. One passenger insisted the captain and several officers shot themselves as the end neared. According to fireman Harry Senior, who provided a *Times* reporter with several observations, most of them suspect that the captain swam to a lifeboat with a child in his arms. After depositing the infant, he took off his lifebelt and said, "I will follow the ship," and did. In fairness to Mr. Senior, he was not the only one who professed to witness something along these lines. The incident, real or imagined, was what many people wanted to believe. It became duly immortalized in a cartoon that ran in some of the more sensational papers. No evidence that the heroic act actually took place emerged at either inquiry.

The *Times's* coverage also abounded with survivor comments about the fates of the famous passengers: how Isidor Straus, owner of Macy's, and wife Ida went down hand in hand; and the scenario of John Jacob Astor gallantly escorting his new nineteen-year-old bride, Madeleine, to a lifeboat. The paper's own description of events at the pier added a serene portrait of the young widow Astor.

Those of lesser social standing tended not to fare as well in the recollections gathered. One unnamed passenger's observation that Chinese stokers jumped into the lifeboats ahead of the women was uncritically cited. Although we do know that several Chinese in steerage did survive, a perusal of the crew list would have shown that none was employed by White Star. The detailed research Van Anda used to plan the coverage was not always in evidence when it came time to verifying statements.

Amidst the numerous claimed observations that strain credibility, we find the measured impressions of Lawrence Beesley. That his statement resides in the middle of page 3 may be a result of the way the presses rolled when all the stories were gleaned, or a deliberate decision not to let his account appear too prominently, lest it diminish reader interest in what others were saying. In any case, the *Times* sensed the credibility of Beesley's words and allowed them to fill four columns. Only the Bride story was more lengthy.

Beesley presented his view of the sequence of events, from collision to rescue. He noted the irony of his being able to get into lifeboat 13, which had sufficient room and, unlike the others, was not limited to women and children (crewmen were permitted to man those boats, in any case). Two points in his account were particularly haunting: the way the ship remained motionless just prior to the final plunge—five minutes by his estimate; and the horrifying scene of those crying out in the freezing water. The same incidents were noted by other survivors, but the understated tenor of Beesley's account gave his description of such moments unmatched power. His portrait of dawn aboard the lifeboat was particularly evocative, with the distant icebergs that appeared through a mist likened to schooners.

The *Times* was obviously aware that this 19 April issue was a journalistic tour de force. At some point they must have also sensed that their news-gathering methods might draw criticism. This was evidenced on pages 7 and 10 in two statements by Marconi. The first contained an admission that both he and Bottomley received assistance from the *Times* in getting to the *Carpathia*. He added that the reporter accompanying them had not planned to board the ship, a statement that must have left the paper's rivals incredulous. However, Marconi did not state how the reporter managed to board or that Bottomley was held back.

In the page 10 article, Marconi began by decrying the lack of lifeboats. He then went on to explain the *Carpathia's* minimal communication on the grounds that she had an old small wireless and only one operator who had his hands full transmitting the names of survivors. Under such circumstances, he noted, the press had to come in second. He did not mention that the aging wireless set belonged to his company, as did the policy to allow single-operator stations. An inkling that both he and the *Times* would have to further explain themselves was suggested in an announcement that appeared on the following page. It noted the arrival in New York of Senator Smith, who was said to be heading for the *Carpathia,* and mentioned the soon-to-be convened inquiry.

Despite the controversy surrounding the creation of the 19 April 1912 *New York Times,* a controversy of more concern to the other papers and Senator Smith than to the public, this issue has become a classic. Not since the exposure of Boss Tweed had the paper been so high profile, and this time the visibility was international.

Several years later, when Van Anda went to London and visited the offices of Lord Northcliffe's *Daily Mail,* the editor on duty produced a copy of the renowned issue of the *Times* and said, "We keep this as an example of the greatest accomplishment in news reporting." Even today, it remains the most important single issue contributing to the establishment of the *Times* as a global voice.

9

Why?

For 15–19 April, the primary goal of newspapers covering the sinking of the *Titanic* was to gather and present all possible information pertaining to *what* had happened. After the *Carpathia's* arrival and launch of the American Senate's inquiry, the burning question became *why.*

Answers gradually emerged, but they were beset with controversy and were sometimes contradictory. Not surprisingly, public fascination was relentless. In the New York press, coverage of the story did not leave the front pages of the *Times* until 3 May; the *Tribune,* 29 April; the *Herald,* 28 April; the *World,* 5 May; and the *Evening Sun* and the *Journal,* 4 May. If we also include Astor's funeral and the disposition of his estate, then *Titanic*-related stories lingered in the headlines of most New York papers until 9 May.

Although it was the 19 April *Times* that caught the eye of the world, other New York dailies had also seized the moment afforded by the *Carpathia's* arrival. A brief consideration of what they emphasized might be appropriate here before we consider follow-up coverage based on the Senate inquiry that began the same day.

The *Tribune* went with a headline announcing that the collision had occurred at 21 knots. A subheadline noted that the men in first and second classes remained calm during the crisis, while Italians had to be shot to keep order. Needless to say, New Yorkers of Italian extraction did not take kindly to this bit of xenophobic reporting, based as it was on contradictory testimony. In a later article, Colonel Archibald Gracie, a devotee of history and future author of *The Truth About the Titanic* (1913), claimed no one was shot, although a revolver was fired once. Another set of comments had Dr. Washington

Dodge insisting that it was two men in first class trying to get into a boat who where shot by an officer, who then turned the gun on himself. One of the most reliable witnesses, Lawrence Beesley, did not mention a shooting; his observations were recounted in the *Tribune,* but at half the length of those in the *Times.*

The *Herald* went with a headline citing Astor's heroism in helping his wife and several other female passengers gain access to the boats. Consistent with the excellent visuals the paper had been presenting since the beginning of the week, the front page contained a sequence drawing by seventeen-year-old *Titanic* survivor Jack Thayer, showing the ship breaking in two before the final plunge. This thesis, which had few adherents among survivors at the time, became almost completely discounted in subsequent decades. In 1985 Robert Ballard's discovery of the wreck showed the *Titanic* indeed to be in two pieces, thereby affirming the keenness of Thayer's perception. On page 2 there was another impressive visual scoop: five photographs taken from the *Carpathia* showing the lifeboats coming alongside and survivors being taken aboard.

The accompanying articles chronicled details of Astor's gallantry and the less laudable comportment of Ismay. The tenor of the Ismay pieces suggested that no matter how he obtained his place in a boat, he should not have. In an interview with one of the *Carpathia*'s officers, who wished to remain anonymous, the man claimed to have observed Ismay, during the passage to New York, "demanding" food and "forcing" two dollars on the steward who brought it to him. In a more positive vein, the paper noted that Ismay had declared his support for the inquiry and his willingness to answer formally all questions. The last notable personality whose behavior was discussed was Captain Smith. He was said to have remained at his post while shouting commands through a megaphone; the widely cited incident of his rescue of a child was not part of the *Herald*'s commentary.

A photograph of the *Carpathia* docking graced the front page of the *World,* along with estimates of the death toll and the contention that "Nearer, My God To Thee" was the *Titanic*'s musical finale. This song was also deemed to be *the* one by the *Herald.* (The *Times,* however, on the basis of the testimony of their star witness, Harold Bride, leaned toward the Episcopal hymn, "Autumn," with its haunting line, "Hold me up in mighty waters.")

Today, the story of the band—or bands, since there was a quintet led by Wallace Hartley, as well as a trio for the Café Parisien—and the final song, is often pondered when the sinking is discussed. Walter Lord, in his recent *Titanic* update, *The Night Lives On,* devoted an entire chapter to it. In my research travels I have been told of the existence of a monument to the *Titanic*'s bandsmen in Broken Hill, New South Wales, Australia, at least 600 miles from the sea, and been informed that they have been further immortalized in a best-selling Norwegian novel, Erik Fosnes Hansen's *Psalm Upon the Journey's End*.

As to the final song, several schools of thought prevail. Survivor Eva Hart, in a recent television interview, insisted it was "Nearer, My God, to Thee" and that hearing the hymn today still gives her chills. Doubters argue that, although the hymn may have been played earlier on the fatal day, it is unlikely that such a somber piece would have been selected during the evacuation, since the purpose of the band playing was to keep people's spirits up. Proponents of this view favor an upbeat popular selection, such as "Songe d'Automne."

Walter Lord seems inclined in this direction. He disqualifies the hymn, "Autumn," on the grounds of its obscurity and the fact that hymns are usually known by their first lines, not by the titles of the melodies on which they are based; in the case of the rarely performed "Autumn," the lines would be "Guide Me, O Thou Great Jehovah." He also invokes further evidence against the favorite of *Titanic* movies, "Nearer, My God To Thee," by noting that it has three different melody possibilities, two used in Britain, one in the United States. How could both American and British survivors therefore claim with certainty this was the piece they heard?

Subsequent *World* coverage focused on the personalities involved. Mention was made here, too, of the noble behavior of Isidor and Ida Straus, owners of Macy's, who died together as an alternative to being separated.

The paper's reportage of the actions of Ismay surrounded him with a question mark. On one hand, he was quoted as saying that White Star would do its utmost for the survivors and their families and that he welcomed the Senate inquiry. On the other hand, the paper noted that he "snapped back angrily" at reporters who asked if he left in the first boat, claiming instead to have been in the last. A few pages later, several sailors (the name Jack Williams is mentioned) stated they saw Ismay leave on the first boat, a claim that the later inquiry would in no way support. Adding to the loss column of its Ismay scorecard, the *World* noted how he, along with other employees of the line, had their plans for an immediate departure from New York thwarted by Senator Smith.

Ismay's case was presented somewhat more matter-of-factly in the *Sun*, although readers probably still ended up thinking the worst. The coverage also included the requisite barrage of interviews with survivors willing to recount their experiences. This was prefaced by the most detailed assessment to appear in any New York paper regarding the landing of the *Carpathia*, replete with descriptions of the confusion and sadness that reigned.

All New York newspapers of 19 April mentioned the inquiry that would begin that same day. However, only Hearst's *Journal*, taking its mandate as an evening publication seriously, included extended testimony. (A brief summary appeared in the *Evening Sun.*) Initially held at the Waldorf-Astoria, the proceedings would be moved to Washington, DC, on Monday, the 22nd. At the Waldorf, Ismay was the first to testify.

The disaster's most notorious survivor presented events from his point of view, a view that Senator Smith would have cause to challenge in the days to come. According to the *Journal*, Ismay opened with a lament for the loss. He then went on to note that although he knew of the presence of ice, he was just a passenger and had no say regarding navigational decisions. In defense of White Star, he insisted that the ship was not trying to set a record; in defense of himself, he restated the circumstances of his departure in what he claimed was the last boat. Reporting this testimony was a good beginning for the *Journal*'s second phase of *Titanic* coverage, but not enough to erase the pain caused to so many by the false rescue story it ran initially.

The inquiry generated enormous interest and not just because of the statements made there and the personalities involved. The flamboyant and relentless way Senator William Alden Smith conducted it became an international cause cèlébre, and led to divided attitudes among New York newspapers. The *Times,* initially supportive of the proceedings, soon turned negative. The reason was obvious. In the midst of enjoying global status as the publication of record regarding the tragedy, the paper became implicated in the very events being reported when Senator Smith linked its coverage to the corporate high-handedness he was seeking to expose regarding White Star and Marconi.

Probing the culpability of White Star meant subjecting its managing director, Bruce Ismay to an avalanche of scrutiny. However, if we look dispassionately at the tragedy, it can be seen as one in which nature and culture rather than specific individuals played the major roles: Shakespearean in terms of the drama and values that were played out; un-Shakespearean given the absence of strong central characters whose attributes guided the course of events. Yet the public, then as now, could not abide a tragedy wrought of human failure in which there were no distinct personalities upon whom to lay blame. Ismay, therefore, became the personification of the British Board of Trade and the navigational practices of White Star.

By 20 April, Ismay's initial testimony at the hearing was widely reported. The paper that made the most of it was the *World.* "ISMAY IS GRILLED," read the headline, with a large portrait beneath it. What Ismay had said while testifying was simply not enough for readers of the populist-leaning paper. A reporter followed his every move, and noted that Ismay was pacing, smoking, twitching nervously, and barely able to hold himself together—behaviors that must have led readers into assuming some taint of guilt.

Ismay heightened the negative aura surrounding him when he consented to be interviewed by the *World* reporter. Although declaring that he was just a passenger and that his conscience was clear, he also remarked that the hearing had been unfair, especially to him. Several days later he wisely retracted the statement. Other issues besides the sinking appeared to have been at stake in the paper's accusing portrayal of him, such as the worth of American popular democracy compared to British hereditary privilege. The reporter waxed explicit on this contrast: "His whole makeup denotes a life of ease rather than one of strength, as if he were accustomed to having his own way because it is given to him rather than because he wins it."

Two days later the headline read, "ISMAY PUTS RESPONSIBILITY ON DEAD CAPTAIN." Since there was a modicum of sympathy for Captain Smith—the 20 April *World* had quoted someone claiming to have witnessed the child rescue incident—to render such an accusation undoubtedly aroused more public ire. But as might be expected, the text of the accompanying article did not quite match the implications of the headline. Rather than blame the captain for the tragedy, Ismay merely restated how the skipper, not he, was responsible for the speed and route the ship followed, and that as far as he understood it, the decisions made were quite normal under the circumstances.

Even the *Times,* less prone to sensationalizing, realized that Ismay-bashing was the theme of the week. The paper's 21 April summary of the hearing cited a wireless message from the *Carpathia* urging White Star to make the *Cedric* ready to spirit Ismay and the other company survivors back to England as soon as possible. Its signature of "YAMSI," a code name using a simple letter reversal that fooled no one, served to make his actions all the more suspicious. Ismay's explanation only made matters worse: that he was concerned for the welfare of the crew lest they "get into trouble" while in the United States. The paper further compounded his image problem by citing an earlier interview in which he described the inquiry as "brutally unfair."

Subsequent witnesses called to testify were mostly crew. They were suspicious regarding the direction in which the senator would lead them and as a result were somewhat retentive. Another factor that must have weighed on their minds was the possible repercussions that might follow statements made at the inquiry, when they would have to face their employer, White Star, and the British press, after the voyage home.

It was widely felt among White Star employees that Senator Smith was not a man knowledgeable enough to conduct such an investigation. A midwesterner from Michigan, his maritime knowledge was minimal, but he took nothing for granted. Although some of the questions he asked about seafaring practices reflected a landlubber's ignorance, they often yielded information that enlightened an American public uninformed in such matters. The more knowledgeable British public was fueled by a press that derided him constantly and often referred to the inquiry as a "farce." No doubt his dramatic style and populist sentiments repeatedly grated against their traditional reserve.

Over the past several decades the weight of *Titanic* scholarship, even in Britain, has tended to regard the senator and his inquiry with increasing respect. Flamboyant he may have been, but conscientious and thorough as well. No one has done more to redeem this episode in American history than psychologist and historian Wyn Craig Wade. His *The Titanic: End of a Dream,* first published in 1979, contains an extended profile of the Michigan senator and a detailed account of the hearing.

While the British press questioned the legitimacy of the senator's "farce," their American counterparts took a suspicious attitude toward several witnesses from Britain. It was felt that their discomfort with the proceedings would prompt them to reveal less than they knew. As lead-off man, Ismay probably set the tone for this attitude, but it was later exacerbated when the person took the stand whom many construed to be the one most informed to comment on the disaster: Second Officer Charles Lightholler.

When Lightholler was queried, he told the amazing story of his own survival. At one point the senator asked when he left the ship. The response was that he did not. In a quick retort that Lightholler must have appreciated, the senator asked if it was the ship that left him. "Yes," was the reply. Most of the other questions addressed navigational practices and lifeboat capacity and procedure. Nearly all New York papers intimated that getting straight answers from him was like pulling teeth. When safely home, Lightholler would repeatedly denounce the aims and leadership of the investigation.

It did not help Lightholler's cause to be preceded on the stand by Captain Arthur Rostron of the *Carpathia*. In terms of seamanship, Rostron's wisdom and actions during the disaster seemed the embodiment of informed heroism, which earned him a Congressional Medal of Honor. The press inevitably weighed Lightholler's testimony against Rostron's and found it evasive and imbued with suspect judgment. The question of judgment was most apparent when the issue was broached as to why Lightholler lowered boats with so few people in them. The response—that he did not want to overload the tackle and was not sure the ship was doomed in any case—was cited in a number of papers, most notably the 20 April *Times*. Nevertheless, his words were deemed less than convincing.

The issue of Lightholler's judgment emerged again several days later. On 24 April, the headline of the *World* read, "LOOKOUT SWEARS GLASSES WOULD HAVE ALLOWED HIM TO SPOT BERG." The reference was to binoculars, not eyeglasses, and to Frederick Fleet, who spotted the berg from the crow's nest on the fatal night and then relayed his observation to the bridge. In testifying before the hearing, he stated that he could have spotted the ice earlier and in time to avoid it had the crow's nest been supplied with binoculars. It was an intriguing hypothesis, and the press made the most of it. Such a small innocuous item, the presence of which might have prevented the disaster of the century. Thoughts come to mind now, perhaps they did in 1912 as well, of Shakespeare's famous example whereby the absence of a nail leads to the loss of a horseshoe, then the horse, the battle, and eventually the kingdom.

Why were no binoculars issued to the lookouts? Ironically, they were, from Belfast to Southhampton, and to lookouts on most other White Star vessels. For the *Titanic*'s transatlantic voyage they were recalled and assigned to officers on the bridge. Fleet and the other lookouts requested them back and were refused. The officer denying them: Lightholler.

When questioned about the incident, Lightholler shrugged it off, claiming that overreliance on binoculars can be a liability in maintaining a sharp vigil. Other experts such as Admiral Peary (the renowned polar explorer, who must have had some familiarity with icebergs) disagreed. His opinion on the issue was voiced in an interview in the 24 April *World*. What was not done then, and would probably occur in the case of a similar incident today, was to test the available binoculars. Their ability to spot a distant iceberg under low-light conditions would depend less on power and more on the aperture of the primary lens and overall optical quality.

Another larger and more controversial story soon eclipsed the binocular episode. It was foreshadowed by Fourth Officer Joseph Boxhall's testimony of 22 April. In some papers that evening and in others the next day, amidst his reported comments on ice, navigation, and lifeboat evacuation, we find the unsettling observation that he had spotted a ship approximately five miles from the *Titanic*. Boxhall, who had binoculars, saw both her port and starboard lights and tried to signal her using Morse lamp. There was no acknowledgment of his call nor to the distress rockets he was periodically launching. Subsequent witnesses corroborated his story. Since it was assumed that any such ship would have certainly responded, the incident remained puzzling, but was soon supplanted in the press by commentary on other issues.

Then, news from Boston. The Leyland liner *Californian* had docked there on the 19th and rumors were spreading among the crew that some of them had seen a distant ship and rockets the night the *Titanic* went down. Captain Lord, in a press statement (in New York it appeared in the 24 April *World*), attributed such talk to the crew's overactive imagination. The next day the *Boston American* dropped a bombshell—a legitimate scoop for a Hearst paper at last—by printing the statement of Ernest Gill, an assistant engineer on the *Californian*.

Gill recounted seeing a ship's lights that night, as well as rockets indicating "a vessel in distress." He also told of overhearing conversations about the incident among several officers in the morning. The day after this statement appeared he was whisked off to Washington, along with Captain Lord and several crewmen. Although Gill had been paid $500 for his story (a precedent already set by Bride and Cottam with the *Times*), Senator Smith found it convincing enough to have all those involved testify formally. In reporting the story, the *Times* made explicit mention of the $500 paid to Gill. The paper was still smarting from the negative feelings aroused by its payoff to Bride and Cottam, and wanted to emphasize that it was not alone in engaging in the practice.

The statement was read to the investigative committee and Gill was questioned. Both seemed credible. Captain Lord was next. He mentioned the distant ship and that an effort had been made to contact her via Morse lamp. Then he noted how shortly after he had retired for the night, he was informed that a rocket might have been spotted, whereupon he asked the duty officer to keep morsing. Eventually the ship in question disappeared and was assumed to have sailed off.

Cyril Evans, the *Californian*'s wireless operator, was then called. Although asleep during the sinking, he told the committee of hearing talk about rockets the next morning. He also answered "No" to a question that hovers over the *Californian* incident to this day: Did he know why he was not called to his station by the captain when the first rocket was sighted?

Press coverage of Captain Lord was unsparing and public reaction swift. He became the scapegoat of the moment, easing for a time the burden of criticism from the shoulders of Ismay. The incident was also one in which the British Board of Trade Inquiry, although approaching its investigation quite differently, would concur with the American Senate assessment.

Of the many issues raised at the inquiry (far more than can be considered here), the *Times*'s exclusive with Marconi's wireless operators was one that made the press itself part of the very chain of events it was mandated to cover. When these interviews were initially published, the importance of the two operators in the disaster scenario became unquestionably clear. But since their accounts had been a *Times* exclusive, other papers seemed not to have given the men the coverage they deserved . . . until Senator Smith put them on the stand, along with Marconi and his chief New York engineer, Frederick Sammis.

In the 21 April *World*, there was extensive critical commentary on Bride's statement to the committee and his exclusive to the *Times*. To further cast him in a negative light, the paper cited his repeated denunciation of the wireless operators aboard the U.S. Navy's *Chester*. A subheadline then informed readers that Uncle Sam's operators are equal to the best, and a substantial article marshalled evidence to prove the contention. The *Herald* of the same day built its case against the *Times* by discussing the Sammis Marconigram urging the operators to keep their mouths shut and to hold their stories. These journalistic critiques were only possible because the senator had done his wireless homework and asked probing questions.

When Smith put Marconi on the stand, the inventor denied arranging for an exclusive, despite the evidence. He also claimed that the messages sent only resulted because he had not been averse to his operators accepting payment for any stories once their duties were discharged—from whom this payment might derive was, he insisted, of no concern to him. But Smith's research had already uncovered Marconi's liaison of several years with the *Times*. To the paper's readers and rivals, this must have come as no surprise: as noted earlier, a Marconi section regularly supplied the *Times* with European news; and when the inventor elected to speak out on this or that issue, the *Times* was often his venue of choice.

Throughout his interrogation of witnesses regarding the wireless collusion incident, Senator Smith was more concerned in exposing the Marconi Company's corporate machinations than he was in indicting the journalistic ethics of the *Times*. Rival papers tended to follow the opposite course. Marconi was a hero whose questionable judgment in this instance merited no more than a firm slap on the wrist, although the 25 April *Journal* registered a harsher verdict. The *Times*, on the other hand, was a competitor that had transgressed. Accusations of profiting from a tragedy were particularly vehement from the camps of Pulitzer and Hearst.

The *Times*'s reaction was twofold. First, it sought to defend the actions that had yielded the exclusive, and then it waged a campaign to discredit the senator. In the 26 April issue an extended commentary argued that Bride, injured and having lost all his belongings (violins resound between the lines) gave the interview only after all his duties had been discharged. The commentary continued by challenging Smith's contention that the Bride story was an attempt on the part of the paper to keep news of the *Titanic* "away from the world in general."

Rather than defend Marconi directly, the paper went on to reprint statements given at the hearing in which he defended himself from Smith's accusations. The senator's probing questions and occasionally caustic responses to Marconi's answers were, of course, omitted. The discussion came to a close by indirectly challenging Smith's competence to lead such an inquiry, citing criticisms that appeared in the British press. The *Times* was particularly derisive of Smith's question to Fifth Officer Lowe regarding the composition of an iceberg. It had been posed earlier to Boxhall, and the exchange showed that Smith was clearly aware that debris other than ice might be involved. The *Times*, however, preferred to convey the impression that he was oblivious to the obvious.

In the days that followed, the *Times* increased its Smith-bashing. Editorials continued to question the senator's competence and to malign his methods. The 29 April issue reported, on the basis of shaky evidence, that fellow senators on the committee insisted he abandon the investigation or they would resign. It is not difficult to construe this story as another effort on the part of the *Times* to deflect the mounting criticism to which it was being subjected, especially since the article that followed contains a denial that the paper had behaved conspiratorially and monopolistically in securing the Bride interview.

Ironically, the *Times* had supported Smith before he exposed its collusion with Marconi. In going on the attack, the paper also wanted to convey a sense that other members of the press shared their view of the senator's ineptness. Several late April subheadlines cited British newspaper accounts decrying the hearing and its chairman. The accompanying *Times* articles—one suspects the genius of Carr Van Anda—cleverly bemoaned the bad impression of America the hearing was imparting to the rest of the world.

The anti-Smith campaign was too obviously self-serving to win many supporters among the public or rival papers. The *Times* would eventually abandon its effort to discredit him, but only after one last sarcastic volley. A subheadline on the front page of the 1 May issue read, "LONDON OFFERS SMITH A JOB." The article described how an English music hall had invited him to lecture on navigation and safety at sea, for a price he could name. The impression conveyed was that the offer was taken seriously, since his formal decline was reprinted.

Smith's concluding statement regarding the inquiry took place before the Senate on 18 May. With flowery rhetoric that avoided holier-than-thou moralizing, he found the British Board of Trade overly lax in its shipping regulations (especially those pertaining to the number of lifeboats on giant liners), and the White Star Line less than diligent, given its failure to both test available lifesaving gear and to establish drills and stations. On the personal side, Captain Smith should have been more vigilant given the conditions; ditto for Captain Lord of the *Californian*. The Senator concluded by calling for more stringent regulations for commercial shipping as well as for wireless—Marconi was spared the embarrassment of being mentioned by name in the second instance.

The American press response was overwhelmingly positive—the British press was mixed, but mostly negative. Perhaps most laudatory was the coverage in the Hearst papers, which was accompanied by a personal letter of congratulations from the new Czar himself. Perhaps so gracious a response concealed a sense of relief: that it was the *New York Times* collusion with Marconi that had been the target of Smith's one foray into media criticism, rather than Hearst's *New York Journal* for its inaccurate reporting of the story during the first week. Even the *Times,* with the hatchet for Smith now buried but probably not forgotten, conceded that his summation, although not informed by maritime expertise, was well-founded in every instance.

FIRST WIRELESS PRESS MESSAGE ACROSS THE ATLANTIC

Signalizing the Opening of the Marconi Service to the Public, and Conveying
a Message of Congratulation from Privy Councillor Baron Avebury,
Formerly Sir John Lubbock.

THE WESTERN UNION TELEGRAPH COMPANY.

24,000 OFFICES IN AMERICA.   CABLE SERVICE TO ALL THE WORLD.

This Company TRANSMITS and DELIVERS messages only on conditions limiting its liability, which have been assented to by the sender of the following message. Errors can be guarded against only by repeating a message back to the sending station for comparison, and the Company will not hold itself liable for errors or delays in transmission or delivery of Unrepeated Messages, beyond the amount of tolls paid thereon, nor in any case where the claim is not presented in writing within sixty days after the message is filed with the Company for transmission.
This is an UNREPEATED MESSAGE, and is delivered by request of the sender, under the conditions named above.
ROBERT C. CLOWRY, President and General Manager.

RECEIVED at 819 Sixth Ave. Corner 46th St.

TELEPHONE: 8007 BRYANT.

1B Lr Sn   Dh & 53 Collect   D,, P R, Land lines,

London Via Marconi Wireless:Glace   Bay N S Oct 17th,

Times, New York..

This message marks opening transatlantic wireless handed

Marconi company for transmission Ireland Breton limited 50 words

only send one many messages received Times signalise event

quote trust introduction wireless more closely unite people states

Great Britian who seem form one Nation though under two Governments

and whose interests are really identical.

Avebury Marshall .... 1210 Am Oct17th

ALWAYS OPEN.   **MONEY TRANSFERRED BY TELEGRAPH.**   **CABLE OFFICE.**

The above message was immediately followed by others which appear in
another column of The Times this morning.

MARCONI CONGRATULATES THE NEW YORK TIMES

GLACE BAY, NOVA SCOTIA, Oct. 17.—Mr. Marconi says: "Congratulate New York Times
on having received first westward press message."

FROM THE PRIME MINISTER OF FRANCE.

WEST STRAND, London, Oct. 17, via Marconi Wireless Telegraph to Glace Bay, N. S.—THE NEW YORK TIMES Paris correspondent forwards to me the following message for transmission across the Atlantic by Marconi wireless telegraph:

"Dans l'inauguration de prodigieux mode de communication mis désormais à leur disposition, les deux grandes républiques ne peuvent que trouver une heureuse occasion de se féliciter et de formuler les voeux les plus cordiaux pour le maintien de la paix dans le travail pour le bonheur des peuples dans la solidarité."
" CLEMENCEAU."

[Translation.]

In the inauguration of the marvelous means of communication put at their disposition from this time forward, the two great Republics could not but find it a happy occasion to congratulate themselves and to express the most cordial wishes for the maintenance of peace in the work for the happiness of the people in the joint responsibility.
CLEMENCEAU.

The 18 October 1907 *New York Times* proudly announces its business liaison with
Marconi for transatlantic wireless news.

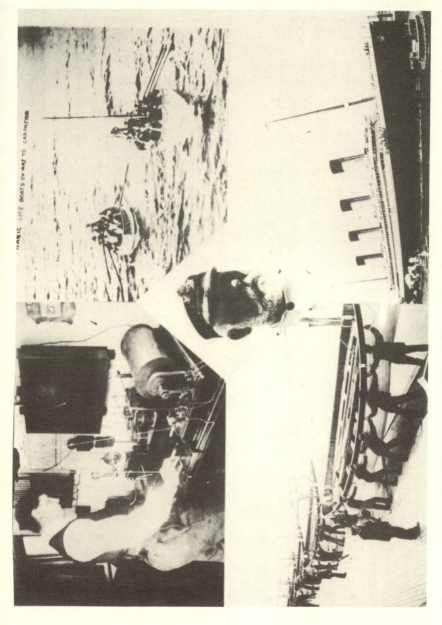

Photo montage with the *Titanic*'s captain, E. J. Smith, at the center. Clockwise from top left: a wireless operator receiving information about the sinking; two *Titanic* lifeboats approaching the *Carpathia*; starboard-bow shot of the *Titanic* leaving Southampton; a lifeboat drill (not from the *Titanic*). Reproduced from the collections of the Library of Congress.

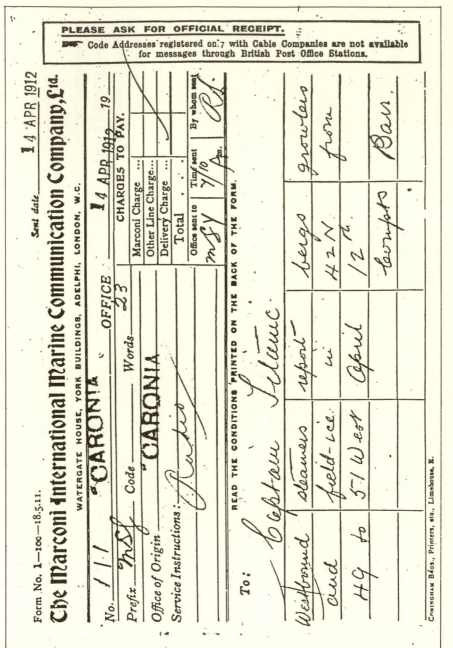

Telegram of an ice warning sent from the *Caronia* to the *Titanic*, 14 April 1912. Reprinted with permission of White Star Publications.

A second telegram of an ice warning transmitted from the *Amerika* to the *Titanic*, later in the day on 12 April 1912. Reprinted with permission of White Star Publications.

200---26/4/12.   MIMCC.5

Forwarding Charges _____ Delivered or sent date 14ᵗʰ Apl.

SERVICE FORM.

THE MARCONI INTERNATIONAL MARINE COMMUNICATION Co., Ltd.

Office Rec'd from	Time Rec'd	By whom Received	Office sent to	Time Sent	By whom Sent
Copy	11·10 P.m.		24 2 22 W	m.	

No. H Baltic, _____ OFFICE _____ 191__

Prefix _____ Code _____ Words _____

From _Titanic_   To _Baltic_

41. 46 N

50. 14 W.

Sinking wants

immediate

assistance

243 off Pos

Wireless message of the _Titanic_'s plight as received by the _Baltic_ on 14 April 1912. Reprinted with permission of White Star Publications.

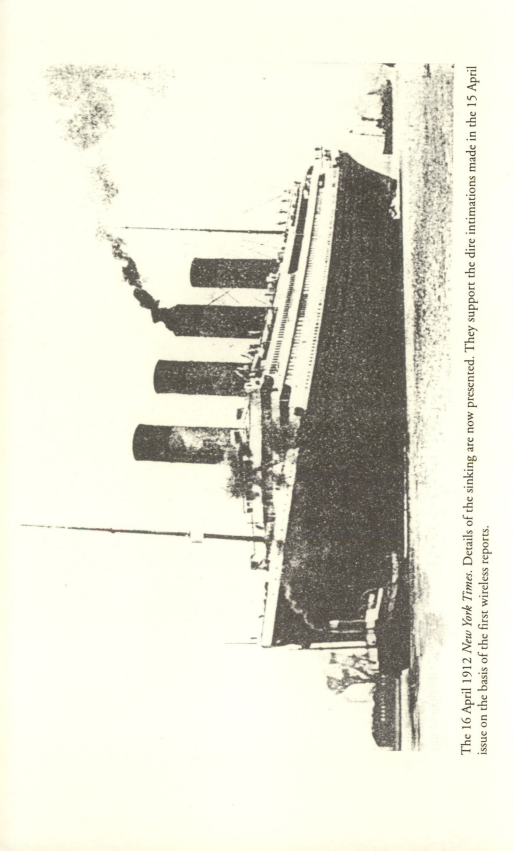

The 16 April 1912 *New York Times*. Details of the sinking are now presented. They support the dire intimations made in the 15 April issue on the basis of the first wireless reports.

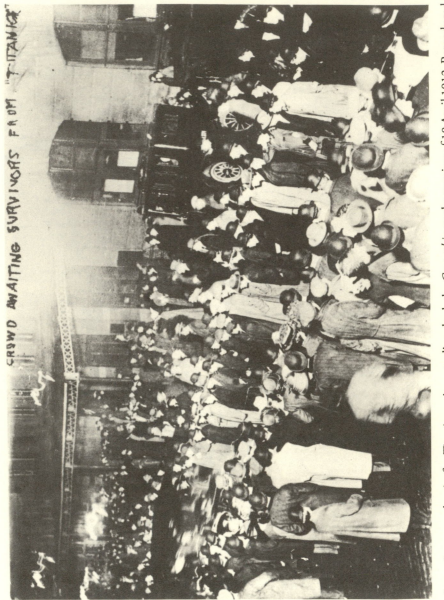

An anxious crowd waits for *Titanic* survivors to disembark the *Carpathia* on the evening of 18 April 1912. Reproduced from the collections of the Library of Congress.

An injured Harold Bride, the *Titanic's* second wireless operator, leaving the *Carpathia* on 19 April 1912. Reproduced from the collections of the Library of Congress.

The U.S. Senate Committee investigating the disaster questions the *Titanic*'s most notorious survivor, Bruce Ismay (hand on chin), chairman of the White Star Line and President of International Mercantile Marine. Reproduced from the collections of the Library of Congress.

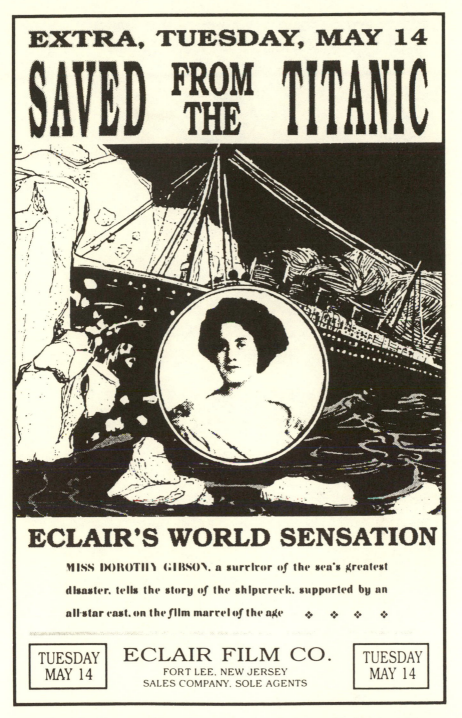

Poster from the film, *Saved from the Titanic*, released one month after the sinking.

Paintings from Canadian artist Steve Gouthro's 1990 interpretive series, "Vestiges of the *Titanic*." Although inspired by photographs of the wreck site, the paintings evoke aspects of the tragedy which transcend what photographs alone can represent. Reprinted with permission of Steve Gouthro.

Part IV

DISASTER AS METAPHOR

The dream of reason produces monsters.

—Goya

As the furor over the *Titanic's* demise subsided in the press, commentary on the event resurfaced in essays, poetry, and film. Later decades would see the topic broached in fiction, drama, music, and, most recently, visual art, radio, and television. Through these various media, the status of the disaster has been transformed from a devastating news story, tinged with unanswered questions and the assumed accountability of agencies such as the White Star Line, to an inclusive metaphor of technological hubris and cultural extravagance. What began as an accident of history has become a story of one of its enduring moral lessons—a real-life counterpart to high tragedy in literature. The works of Sophocles, Shakespeare, and Melville seem as appropriate to understanding what happened to the *Titanic* as do the conclusions of any purely historical study.

The emergence of the *Titanic* disaster as one of the dominant moments in western cultural history can be seen to have taken place in three phases bounded by the following years: 1912–54; 1955–84; and 1985 to the present.

Phase one began with a series of responses to the event by several luminaries of the Edwardian literary world, among them Joseph Conrad, George Bernard Shaw, Arthur Conan Doyle, and Thomas Hardy. Cinema also entered the scene at this point and in each subsequent decade would contribute significantly to *Titanic* discourse. The 1930s saw a for-

midable rendering of the tragedy when Canadian E.J. Pratt embraced it
in a lengthy narrative poem. The final event of phase one occurred in
1953, with the release of the Twentieth-Century Fox production, *Titanic*.
Although those first three decades following the disaster saw nothing to
rival the *Titanic* mania that would come later, interest was consistently
maintained despite, or perhaps in part because of, the greater horror of
two world wars, the Holocaust, and Hiroshima.

Phase two began with the 1955 publication of Walter Lord's remarkable book, *A Night to Remember*. It soon inspired an adaptation for television and prompted that medium's continued interest in the *Titanic*.
Three years later Rank Productions of Great Britain released the movie *A
Night to Remember*. It still stands as the definitive cinematic telling of the
story and the prototype and finest example of the disaster-film genre.
The sixties saw the humble beginnings of the Titanic Historical Society,
which has grown into a 5,000 member international organization and
major information center for *Titanic* research. The seventies ended with
a lavish made-for-television melodrama, *S.O.S. Titanic*, and speculation
that the wreck might be found. The eighties opened with *Raise the Titanic* (1980), a $40 million film that quickly bombed, as did three soon-
to-follow attempts to locate the wreck by Texas oil millionaire Jack
Grimm.

In 1985, Robert Ballard's successful expedition to find the *Titanic*
began phase three. The discovery unintentionally set an agenda for events
to the present. They include later expeditions to salvage the wreck and
the ensuing controversy; the opening of an inquiry into the "*Californian*
incident," based on new evidence as to the position of the *Titanic* in
1912; and the giant-screen IMAX film, *Titanica*, still in release as of this
writing. As the century draws to a close and we continue to interrogate
the limits of appropriate technology and conceits of western civilization,
interest in the why and wherefore of the great ship's fate shows no sign
of waning.

10

Responses and Renderings in Literature

By the third week of May 1912, the tempest in the press created by the *Titanic* had gradually subsided. The American Senate hearing had been over for almost a month and the British Board of Trade's version was in the throes of folding its tent. Testimony had been given by eyewitnesses, maritime experts, and those with both credentials. Journalists had editorialized endlessly, as had the general public in countless conversations.

Those of us from the first wave of the post-war baby boom sometimes reminisce by posing the question: where were you when you heard the news that President Kennedy had been shot? Many of us remember. Some of us also recall that we could talk of little else for days, even weeks, after. And so it was following the *Titanic* disaster.

The tragedy was without precedent, not in terms of loss of life but with respect to how it illustrated the unimaginable convergence of so many factors. The old adage about truth being stranger than fiction must have seemed appropriate. After the two hearings, there was a sense that the loss of the *Titanic* was not just a devastating accident whose painful memory would eventually recede but also a scar on the very soul of western civilization. One element that made it so unsettling was the way the cast of characters in the drama were deployed. Technology and nature shared the lead, with individual personalities assigned to supporting roles—a reversal of the way major historical events were usually played out. Never had Emerson's observation that "Things are in the saddle and ride mankind" rung so true.

After a month, the tragedy had exhausted the efforts of journalists to chronicle its full implications, and historians were no better equipped for the task. But almost immediately, and in every decade since, artists working in various genres began adding their impressions. The literary tradition has been exceptionally prolific. Writers whose expertise is tragedy, fate, and individual responsibility have contributed provocative insights. One of the first such commentaries was an essay by George Bernard Shaw in the *Daily News and Leader* on 14 May 1912. It put him on a collision course with another powerful literary voice of the time, Sir Arthur Conan Doyle.

Shaw called his piece "Some Unmentioned Morals," and in it he accused both the press and public of failing to face directly the reasons for and consequences of the tragedy. Instead of an outpouring of profound sympathy for the victims and a dispassionate reflection on the circumstances of the sinking, what had come to the fore was misinformation and false heroism couched in "outrageous romantic lying." Employing a baroque and often sarcastic style, Shaw claimed that British reaction to the event was underscored by a hidden agenda of face-saving and national pride. Too much, he insists, had been attributed to fate and not enough to negligence.

Shaw went on to question the wisdom of women and children first, although not its nobility, and then scornfully noted how it was violated in the boat of Lady Duff Gordon, which had ten men and two women. Obviously no fan of Captain Smith, Shaw resented vehemently the depictions of him as cool and brave in the crisis, depictions that evoked the image of Nelson; had the captain done his job properly, he would have remained anonymous. The officers were also critiqued, not for acting ignobly but for being all too human and then later portrayed as heroic. He cited the case of Lowe versus Ismay in this context, whereby the fifth officer, when supervising the loading of a lifeboat, was given some unwelcomed advice from the managing director of the line, whom he promptly told to "Go to hell."

Leaving no popular image of the ship sacred, Shaw made reference to news stories about the band playing "Nearer, My God To Thee." Obviously informed by later testimony from the hearings, he noted that what was played were upbeat ragtime tunes to avoid a panic. While this was going on, vital information was being withheld from the passengers, especially foreigners in third class. Their alleged unruly behavior was, for him, exaggerated by the press in an effort to highlight the allegedly more admirable reactions that came from those of English descent.

In the 20 May issue of the same paper, came a biting challenge from Sir Arthur Conan Doyle. His essay chastised Shaw for accusing everyone of lying while basing those accusations on false assumptions. If Shaw had thoroughly assessed the situation, instead of selecting evidence to confirm his prejudices, he would have noted how the lifeboat that left after the one cited had sixty-five women and five men. Needless to say, Sir Arthur was doing some selection of his own, since the actual ratio of male to female survivors was just over one to three.

With respect to Captain Smith, Shaw was accused of confusing public sympathy for an honored seaman with approval of his navigational decisions; one mistake should not undo completely an otherwise illustrious career. Sir Arthur went on to note how the captain gave up his lifebelt and eventually swam with a child to a boat he himself refused to enter. This latter event became one of the enduring *Titanic* legends, and, although never verified, it appeared in a widely seen news cartoon. As for the alleged comparisons of Captain Smith to Nelson, this point prompted Sir Arthur to offer £100 to the Fabian Society (the socialist group in which Shaw played a prominent role) for any convincing journalistic evidence of it.

The incident of Lowe versus Ismay was regarded by Sir Arthur as an act of courageous defiance that put duty ahead of the privilege of rank. He went on to observe that reliable witnesses saw foreigners rush the boats, only to be stopped by an officer's pistol shots. And regarding the band playing to avert panic: was this not a wise decision and should they not be honored for carrying it out? He concluded by minimizing the chauvinism that outraged Shaw, arguing that much would be lost if such expressions of courage and duty were not lauded. Shaw was acknowledged as a "genius," but one who had used his talents to condemn, misjudge, and compound the anguish of the situation.

A lengthy rebuttal came on 22 May. Exuding bravado, Shaw declared that no sane person who had carefully studied his text could disagree with it. Sir Arthur's criticism was deemed a "romantic warm-hearted protest." The great playwright then suggested that the great novelist look into his very own novels for authentic cases of heroism, not to the fabrications of the press. The £100 offer was refused on the grounds that he did not want to unduly deprive a friend. For Shaw, any praise for Captain Smith, whom he contended took a major gamble and lost, diminished the dignity of those captains who do their duty with thoroughness and vigilance. If the *Titanic* had been a military ship, would he not have been subject to a court martial? The response ended by noting that ultimately the great moral loss following the disaster remained the substitution of "aspiring achievement" for "sensational misfortune."

On 25 May Sir Arthur closed the exchange with a brief rejoinder. He denied suggesting that Shaw had lied, only that, despite his brilliance, a clear lack of judgment was evident, along with an insensitivity to the feelings of those involved.

What neither of these two literary titans could have realized at the time was that the issues over which they crossed pens would continue to be debated for decades to come.

A writer far more knowledgeable in maritime affairs entered the arena of commentary when Joseph Conrad aired his views in the May 1912 issue of *The English Review.* His eloquent and highly charged essay, "Some Reflections on the Loss of the *Titanic*," was informed by twenty years of service as a seaman, mate, and master, and by an assiduously gathered collection of newspaper accounts of the disaster.

Conrad's essay expressed an almost mocking attitude toward the U.S. Senate investigation. It was seen as rife with misguided enthusiasm and persistent attention to irrelevant details, such as the number of explosions that came from inside the ship as she was going under. He wondered why these senators did not pursue in this manner the many accidents that occurred in the American railway system. The senators' incompetent performance turned a high drama worthy of Shakespeare into something resembling one of the Bard's comedies. These views echoed the way much of the British press regarded Senator Smith's efforts. They also revealed a rarely seen nationalistic side of Conrad. Especially telling in this regard was his contention that, since the *Titanic* was a British ship wrecked in international waters, the surviving officers should not be accountable to the U.S. or any other foreign government. No mention was made of the fact that the ship was actually owned by International Mercantile Marine, an American trust headed by J.P. Morgan.

Any solace the British Board of Trade might have taken from these remarks would have been quickly overridden by subsequent criticism directed at them. Conrad noted that here was an organization of alleged expertise that was complacent, ill-informed about the design implications of new ships, and susceptible to being pressured by commercial interests. Their greatest oversight in this regard was the regulation basing the number of lifeboats a ship carried on her tonnage, a carryover from a time when the normal maximum for a ship was 10,000 tons—less than a quarter the size of the *Titanic*.

He went on to suggest that the sheer size of the *Titanic,* which some experts thought was a safety feature making her a giant lifeboat, was a liability in that it necessitated handling her more delicately than most smaller vessels. To back this contention, he cited an incident he observed several years earlier in Sydney, Australia, whereby a ship half the size of the *Titanic* gently drifted to her berth and virtually destroyed it. He also noted that the steel plating on giant liners simply could not be made as proportionately strong as it could be for smaller vessels.

Another aspect of the incident with which he showed little patience was the argument by some of the builders that the ship would have survived had she rammed the iceberg directly—a view that implied the seamanship was not as informed as it could have been. True, the *Arizona* a few years before had survived such a collision, but she was less than 5,000 tons and could not, according to Conrad's estimate, have been traveling faster than 14 knots. The "modern blind trust in material and appliances" and commercial pressure to make ships appealing to the highly affluent created an unwieldy monster. She was too large for her purpose as an efficient medium of transportation and, because any free space was assigned to more pleasurable pursuits, inadequately equipped with lifeboats.

In contrast to George Bernard Shaw and Sir Arthur Conan Doyle, who stressed negligent navigation, Conrad's emphasis was on the unseaworthiness of the vessel and the shortsightedness of those who brought her into service. He seemed to imply that the *Titanic*'s course and speed did not, per se, represent an unusual risk. Was Conrad's failure to broach this issue perhaps an indication of this former seaman's loyalty to his maritime brethren? His lament over the way seamen had been forced to modify their routines because of commercial pressures suggested as much.

The essay hinted that seafaring will always have an element of risk associated with it, but that a properly prepared vessel is adequate to most situations. The case of the *Duoro* is mentioned, a ship one-tenth the size of the *Titanic*, which was rammed and sank in fifteen to twenty minutes. Nevertheless, all ten lifeboats were launched, and every passenger, except for one who refused to leave the ship, was saved; the captain and most of the crew perished. Conrad's moral was that technology can fail—as can men—but that men, when given a chance, will prove to be "truer than steel," especially, he noted in an ironic afterthought, the kind of steel used for the bulkheads of modern giant liners.

Conrad's reputation and maritime knowledge led to widespread discussion of his statements and a few challenges. He responded with a sequel in the journal's next issue. In it he refused to retract his criticism of the U.S. Senate investigation, but did add that their motivations, if not their methods, were laudable. The rest of the commentary was given over to a technical dissertation on ship design. He reiterated his point about the inadequacy of the hull plate thickness by making a colorful comparison to the Huntley and Palmer biscuit tin, showing the latter's clear superiority in its strength to size ratio. (Over the years the phrase that has come down is something along the lines of, "the *Titanic* was ripped open like a Huntley and Palmer biscuit tin," a somewhat different analogy from the original.) Given the impossibility of making hull plates as relatively thick and strong as the contrivance of Messrs. Huntley and Palmer, several ways were then suggested for making a ship's transverse bulkheads as watertight as possible. The first prerequisite was to downsize luxury appliances and limit the number of passengers.

As in the previous essay, Conrad again leaned toward solutions using what we would today call appropriate technology. He added to his list of interior design ideas the use of mechanical cranes instead of hand-operated davits for the lifeboats, and also proposed that such boats be equipped with small motors. (Two years later he would face a different challenge, when, in the *Illustrated London News,* he was asked to reflect on the collision between the *Storstad* and the *Empress of Ireland.* This incident sank the latter in just over fifteen minutes, taking a thousand lives. Navigational error, *not* ship technology, was the culprit. Conrad did not hesitate to address this question, and his response showed considerable sympathy for both captains. Once a seaman. . . .)

Prose was not the only medium the literati employed when reflecting on the disaster. On 14 May 1912, the day George Bernard Shaw's essay appeared in the *Daily News and Leader,* Thomas Hardy stepped on the stage at Covent Garden and recited the evocative strains of his poem, "The Convergence of the Twain" (see Appendixes). It was composed for the occasion, which was a Dramatic and Operatic Matinée in aid of the *Titanic Relief Fund.* Later versions appeared in the *Fortnightly Review* and various collections of his work.

Commemorative verse was a familiar Hardy vehicle. He had written poems in response to anniversaries, the death of friends, and occasionally to reflect on an historical event. In the vast domain of Hardy scholarship, there is little commentary on "The Convergence of the Twain," which is usually regarded as one of his lesser efforts. A notable exception is expressed in a recent study by Joanne Cullen Brown, who regards it as a "brilliant tour de force," ideally suited in style and tone to its subject. Perhaps it is no coincidence that her evaluation postdates the discovery of the wreck and comes at a time when we know more about the ship than ever before. One noteworthy consequence of the poem is that twenty years after it was written it would provide inspiration for Canadian E.J. Pratt's poetic magnum opus, "The *Titanic,*" which we will consider shortly.

The title of Hardy's poem suggests a coming together of the disparate phenomenon. He views the disaster through a wide-angle, almost cosmic, lens, which avoids both sentiment and condemnation. Notably absent is the now-familiar narrative of the voyage as a rudely interrupted celebration of La Belle Epoque and the associated litany of names. Instead, the first half of the poem surveys the physical aftermath of the collision, the *Titanic* interred on the North Atlantic seabed. The images are haunting, pushed toward us slowly, as if we were drifting in this nether world where

Dim moon-eyed fishes near
Gaze at the gilded gear

Hardy's portrait of the wreck describes a still magnificent structure, now "Deep from human vanity," or shorn from the life that created it. The impression is of an enormous corpse being turned, first into a skeleton, and then to dust:

Over the mirrors meant
To glass the opulent
The sea-worm crawls

In stanzas I to V, Hardy takes us to a place that, since the 1985 discovery of the wreck, millions of us have now glimpsed on television and, most recently, in the IMAX film, *Titanica*. Few words have been written since his that more effectively match this visual evidence.

In stanzas VI to IX, we are taken back in time just prior to the collision. Hardy again rejects the standard view, which in this case would have the grandiose ship ramming an inert iceberg. Both the iceberg and the *Titanic* are said to derive from the same "Immanent Will." They are regarded as complementary elements in a cosmological, but not necessarily religious, grand scheme. Culture has given us this "creature of cleaving wing" for which nature has "Prepared a sinister mate." The two share billing in the drama, they are seen as the "twin halves of one august event," and fated to converge, "By paths coincident."

The use of symmetrical imagery is further extended when Hardy balances his description of the iceberg seemingly growing in size as it looms toward the ship, with the ship as it might have appeared from the iceberg. This point of view is very cinematic—thirty-five years later we find the collision sequence in A *Night to Remember* filmed this way. The poem ends with the collision, which is referred to as a "consummation," a metaphor for both destruction and rebirth. It "jars two hemispheres," again a linking of the destinies of nature and culture, as well as a way of signifying the global impact of the event.

The "Convergence of the Twain" is a remarkably rich work, eerie and powerful. It reflects a trend in late Victorian Romantic literature to regard nature as an awesome and potentially malevolent force. Darwin's view, in which nature is characterized by a "struggle for existence," overrode the tamer notions of Rousseau and Wordsworth, certainly for Hardy. He extends that struggle to include culture challenging nature as a result of human hubris. In the final reckoning, however, nature is all inclusive and must have the last word, in this case voiced at the end of stanza V by the "moon-eyed" fish surveying the wreck, who inquire: " 'What does this vainglorious down here?' . . ."

High verse about the *Titanic,* as penned by Hardy and later E.J. Pratt, is not the only verse. In the popular culture of various folk traditions, the sinking has been the subject of numerous rhymes, ditties, and longer works, the most famous example perhaps being the many versions of the campfire song "It Was Sad When That Great Ship Went Down" (see Appendixes). Two equally notable, if lesser known narratives—"*Titanic* Toast" and "De *Titanic*"—derive from what at first glance would seem to be an unlikely source: the African-American experience.

"*Titanic* Toast" is an oral poem with internal dialogue. Over a dozen versions have been transcribed by researchers and many others no doubt exist. During the early 1970s, Bruce Jackson published a brief compilation, and at the end of the decade Wyn Craig Wade brought the poem to the attention of *Titanic* researchers. Although virtually unknown to whites, "*Titanic* Toast" has been celebrated by millions of African-Americans in the decades since 1912. A "toast" is performed without musical accompaniment, but in a very dramatic and somewhat percussive manner; in this sense it can be seen as a forerunner of rap. Although numerous variations of the poem exist, the overlap in content is high so that reasonable generalizations can be made regarding the dominant themes.

The hero of the poem is named "Shine," a seemingly odd choice since this was the white man's generic pejorative label for a black male, yet ironically appropriate in that Shine would be the one to outwit white culture during its supreme moment of folly. He works in the hold, probably as a stoker, sees the damage created by the collision and tries to inform the captain, who ignores him. Shine then utters several profanities, dives overboard, and starts swimming to New York. He does this in front of the *Titanic*'s millionaires, in some versions a "thousand millionaires," who offer him a fortune to come back and save them. He refuses.

In all variants of the story there is also female temptation: a rich man's daughter, the captain's daughter (who is usually depicted as pregnant and unmarried), or a thousand whores. They come up on deck and offer themselves to Shine in an effort to lure him back to the ship to rescue them. Marriage proposals from some of the wealthy women, usually the captain's daughter, are often part of the package. Shine does not yield. In some versions, another black man named Jim (a black everyman to Shine's trickster?) joins Shine in the swim to New York, but succumbs to the allure of the females and returns to the ship and inevitable death.

This temptation sequence is intriguingly reminiscent of one in Homer's *Odyssey*, also in its original form an oral narrative. What the events in "*Titanic* Toast" suggest is an inversion of the encounter between Odysseus and the Sirens. From rocky sea-swept perches, the Sirens use beguiling vocaleses and the promise of sexual rapture in an attempt to lure Odysseus and his crew. Some of the men, like Jim in "*Titanic* Toast," succumb and perish.

Shine swims with boundless energy toward New York, outdistancing (depending on the version) either a shark or a whale—sometimes both. Occasionally the route is circuitous and he winds up in Los Angeles first, but eventually he always gets to New York and receives news of the fate he escaped. Nearly all versions end with Shine inebriated and often in the company of women. This could be interpreted as a return to normal life, with its basic pleasures, sense of social place, and newly acquired wisdom regarding the vulnerability of white civilization.

"*Titanic* Toast" is unusual in the "toast" genre in that it works with an overt theme of black/white racial opposition. The moral lessons that reside in the poem seem straightforward. Neither the white man's money nor his women are worth the risks involved in acquiring them, therefore they should not be aspired to or coveted. The appearance of the captain's unmarried pregnant daughter suggests that even white nobility can transgress. In rejecting her, Shine is rejecting soiled goods and learning that white skin and purity are not synonymous, but only another myth of the oppressor. Finally, as different as "*Titanic* Toast" is from accounts of the sinking in the poetic renderings of "high culture," there is convergence on one fundamental point: arrogant overconfidence in technology can pose a threat to people of all social backgrounds.

One of the ironies of "*Titanic* Toast" is that there were no blacks on the *Titanic,* nor could there have been given the attitudes and laws of the time. This fact is central to the song, "De *Titanic*" (see Appendixes), which was performed and perhaps composed by Leadbelly. It was eventually collected and published by John Lomax during the 1930s.

"De *Titanic*" pivots on the refusal of the *Titanic* to accept as a passenger the great black heavyweight boxing champion, Jack Johnson, who up to that time had defeated all white challengers:

Jack Johnson wanted to get on boa'd;
Captain Smith hollered, "I ain' haulin' no coal."

Although the incident may be fictitious, we do know that despite his fame and money Johnson was often refused access to the venues of white society; one such refusal was passage on a ship, thus giving "De *Titanic*" a partial basis in fact. The lyrics go on to describe the fate of the *Titanic,* replete with a citation of the singing of "Nearer, My God To Thee." After the sinking, Johnson eventually receives news of it and realizes that the denial of his passage was a blessing in disguise. He dances in celebration. This leads to a concluding moral implying, as in the case of "*Titanic* Toast," that what the white man has and does is not always worthy of envy:

> Black man oughta shout for joy,
> Never lost a girl or either a boy.
> Cryin', "Fare thee, *Titanic,* fare thee well."

Although the African-American oral tradition kept the *Titanic* alive as a subject for poetic reflection, it would not re-enter the "high art" world of poetry until 1935. That year saw the publication of "The *Titanic*" by E. J. Pratt, a thirty-page epic often regarded as the preeminent narrative poem by the most renowned poet in twentieth-century Canadian literature.

Pratt (1883–1964), whose first initials are hauntingly identical to those of Captain Smith (Smith was often called "E. J.," but Pratt was usually addressed as "Ned"), had a background that allowed him to have unusual literary access to the story of the *Titanic.* He was born and raised in a Newfoundland fishing community where maritime lore was a staple of everyday conversation. As an adult he became an ordained Methodist minister like his father. Marginal in this profession, as in his social and geographic origins—Newfoundland would not become a part of Canada until 1949—he sidestepped taking up a parish and pursued a doctorate in religious studies. During this academic sojourn he absorbed enough literature in the natural sciences and humanities to become a cosmopolitan intellectual. From 1920–53, Pratt taught English literature at the University of Toronto and was often regarded as Canada's unofficial Poet Laureate. American and British editions of his work have led to a modest but enthusiastic international following, especially in New England, where his seafaring themes are much appreciated.

That Pratt himself deemed "The *Titanic*" a singularly important work in his overall output is attested to in later interviews and in the dedication to his father. No doubt he could have written about the disaster earlier in his career; the event is a rich mine of metaphor, and he had always been on intimate terms with its circumstances. By waiting to write it until mid career, he was able to bring to the task both stylistic maturity and extensive experience in writing about maritime themes.

In numerous Pratt poems leading up to "The *Titanic,*" the ocean and her many moods are staples. Turbulent, dangerous, widow-making waters are often described in a manner that indicates a debt to those Romantic poets who had depicted nature in tempest. Pratt's word-images of storm-tossed seas also evoke the visual renderings of nature in the paintings of the nineteenth-century British Romanticist J.M.W. Turner, although it is uncertain as to whether there was an influence. This tendency to vivify inanimate nature is a frequent theme in Pratt.

Five years before Pratt wrote "The *Titanic*," a major crisis at sea prompted a poem that became an unintentional dress rehearsal for it. In "The *Roosevelt* and the *Antinoe*," he described the perilous attempt of the former to rescue the latter in January 1927 during one of the fiercest storms in North Atlantic history. The poem tells how *Antinoe*, a British grain freighter heading to England from New York—the reverse of the *Titanic*'s direction—is ravaged by snow, sleet, and wind. She loses her lifeboats and her steering and navigational capacities. Listing badly, she sends an intermittent SOS and is located with a direction finder, then lost, and found again by dead reckoning when her wireless gives out. The *Roosevelt* persists in what at times seems like a futile struggle, which claims the lives of two of her crew. The effort eventually succeeds, but by the barest of margins. All twenty-five crewman are taken from the foundering *Antinoe*, and a heroic and avowedly Homeric debt is repaid, since Captain Tose of the *Antinoe* had directed a similar rescue ten years earlier. In researching the poem Pratt did not limit himself to newspaper accounts, but traveled to New York to read the logs of both ships and to interview several crewmen.

In "The *Roosevelt* and *Antinoe*," humanity, reduced in technological means and against all odds, prevails over the cold indifference of nature. Exactly the reverse takes place in "The *Titanic*." The poem chronicles the ship from her launching on 31 May 1911 to her destruction on 15 April 1912. It is written, as are most of Pratt's longer poems, in an ornate style that bespeaks a debt to the Romantics and even Shakespeare. A superficial reading might lead to the impression that his style is anachronistic, but Pratt is so adroit at meshing older language and form with contemporary themes that the result is rarely less than compelling. Conceptual influences include Hardy, Conrad, and Melville. Details regarding events during the voyage seem to have been drawn from survivor Lawrence Beesley's 1912 memoir, *The Loss of SS Titanic*, probably the most consulted account prior to the publication of Walter Lord's *A Night to Remember*.

In the poem, as the ship is completed she becomes the epitome of a boastful achievement. The scene then shifts to Greenland, where Pratt describes how nature crafted and launched the iceberg. He also notes how an omen of the disaster to come occurs as the *Titanic* is leaving Southampton: the ship's suction pulls the *New York* loose from her moorings, resulting in a near collision. This moment of doubt, however, is soon forgotten as we become caught up in the wonder of a vessel that blends power and elegance. Several pages follow in which two distinct themes are played off one another in an effective counterpoint of irony: the sumptuous menu for first-class passengers and the wireless messages warning of ice ahead.

Wireless held a particular fascination for Pratt. He claimed that one of the great moments in his life occurred when he participated in a high-school field trip to Marconi's wireless station near St. John's, Newfoundland. In 1901, he met the inventor, whose presence seemed almost God-like. Shortly after the encounter, Marconi succeeded in bridging the Atlantic with his wireless. One headline following this triumph impressed Pratt then and later when he was composing "The *Titanic*": "No More Losses at Sea." Fate would conspire against this form of hubris as well, by allowing the disaster to take place so close to the scene of Marconi's success and in creating one of history's most famous "so near yet so far" scenarios, when the nearby *Californian* failed to respond.

Midway in the poem, two pages are given over to a description of a poker game and the ensuing conversation among several first-class passengers. The metaphoric implications soon reveal themselves. What seems like a winning hand turns into quite the opposite. A moment later one of the players asks another to order soda and ice. The response is shattering and provides the first indication in the poem that *the* moment has arrived:

> " '*Ice: God! Look—take it through the port-hole—look!*' "

The scene then shifts to the bridge where the sighting is repeated. Queries and speculations among the crew follow the collision. They seem similar to what we find in most accounts unless the poem is heard rather than read, thus making apparent Pratt's superb ear for conversational rhythm.

Although the *Carpathia*'s rescue of the *Titanic*'s survivors is not part of the poem, her valiant and dangerous commitment to get to the disaster as soon as possible is told in a manner that echoes the heroism celebrated in "The *Roosevelt* and *Antinoe*."

As the end of the *Titanic* draws nigh, one scene follows another with cinematic swiftness. The band plays. Lifeboats leave—some orderly, others in confusion. Millionaires maintain their composure. And, as the ship rises for her descent, boilers and bulkheads break apart. When she finally vanishes, Pratt ignores both the chaos of those dying in the water and the terror of the survivors in lifeboats awaiting rescue. Instead, he turns his attention to the iceberg and concludes with a serene portrait of it drifting on a silent sea in the aftermath of the sinking.

Pratt's poem of the disaster was soon followed by novels. In 1938 the German writer Robert Prechtl published *Titanic*, and within two years British and American editions became available. The disaster had not gone unmentioned in previous fiction, but until Prechtl's effort there was no sustained attempt to make it the centerpiece of an extended narrative. Perhaps it took twenty-five years for the event to recede sufficiently into the annals of history for it to become an appropriate stage for the intermingling of real and hypothetical personalities in the creative development of subplots.

Prechtl's novel has never enjoyed a wide following. It remains, despite recent interest in the *Titanic*, a rarely mentioned and hard to find source. The text is both ponderous (368 pages) and excessively deliberate. The author is at least honest regarding the latter, stating in the preface how the facts of the disaster must be transposed to a qualified fictional context to be truly understood. This is a worthy strategy, but most Anglo-American readers would prefer to discover it by engaging the text rather than by plodding through a somewhat academic statement of purpose.

Instead of providing the reader with characters whose lives can be followed intimately, the first two-thirds of the novel intertwines real and fictional personages into a series of theatrical vignettes. The conversations provide an intriguing glimpse into ideas in the air at the time. Most are voiced by the renowned passengers, especially John Jacob Astor. Technology is at the forefront of these exchanges, followed closely by religion and social mores.

Astor's economic machinations are considered separately in several lengthy digressions on prevailing social conditions, circa 1912. He also figures in a scheme to buy the White Star Line from Bruce Ismay, who in turn is committed to winning the Blue Riband for the fastest crossing, which will up the value of the line's stocks and save it from potential bankruptcy. Occasionally, discussion gets around to the rivalry with German commercial shipping, which the arrogant robber barons on board insist must be defeated at all costs. This theme, however, is not as labored in the novel as it would later be in German director Herbert Selpin's 1943 film *Titanic*, which may have been influenced by Prechtl, although the film's credits indicate no affiliation.

The last third of the story occurs postcollision and deals with the evacuation of the ship. Several new characters are introduced, and the theme of British arrogance and overreaching is replayed. Captain Smith is not given a sympathetic portrayal. Amidst the numerous chaotic scenarios aboard the ship during her final moments is an incident of murder followed by a rape described with such startling explicitness that it is hard to imagine it was written in the 1930s and not more recently. We also find a consideration of the valor exhibited by the Marconi operators, the *Californian's* unresponsiveness, and the *Carpathia's* sprint to the rescue.

Time and again Prechtl's facts are wanting or deliberately fabricated, as in the instance of Astor's desire to buy the White Star Line and the widely held misconception that the ship was trying for a record crossing. However, in fairness to Prechtl, *Titanic* scholarship then was not as it is now. Artistic license aside, his effort is still a worthy one, although by the final chapter, the lack of personalities we can identify with, celebrate, or mourn diminishes the success of the book as conventional popular fiction.

Seventeen years after Prechtl's effort, the drama of the *Titanic* was vividly told in a nonfiction bestseller. Walter Lord's *A Night to Remember*, which will be discussed in the next chapter, does everything a good novel does and more and has become a hard act to follow for any writer dealing with the *Titanic*, regardless of his or her literary persuasion. By the end of the 1980s, however, the discovery of the wreck created a new wave of information and interest pertaining to the sinking and its historical context. This occurred at a time when the public's curiosity regarding the late Victorian and Edwardian periods was being stimulated by motion pictures and television dramas. Two novels emerged from this confluence: *Titanic: A Novel*, by Tony Aspler, and Danielle Steel's *No Greater Love*.

Aspler, who is a Canadian and therefore heir to the literary tradition of E.J. Pratt, uses the sinking of the *Titanic* as the extended finale for a melodramatic adventure. His subtext includes themes such as class conflict, the rampant acquisitiveness of the robber barons during the waning years of classical capitalism, and the transference of industrial wealth from Britain to North America.

The novel's protagonist is Henry Blexil, butler to Lord Rutherford and occasional pugilist in the mold of John L. Sullivan. When his lordship goes belly-up because of what appears to be investments—in reality he was swindled—Henry's services are transferred to the family of his employer's former business associate, the brash and unscrupulous American railroad magnate Thadeus Tarr. From his underclass vantage point, Henry witnesses Tarr's brutal suppression of a coal miner's strike in West Virginia and the various machinations that leave Tarr perpetually at the short end of dealings with his arch rival, J.P. Morgan. (As we know by now, Morgan also controls International Mercantile Marine, which in turn owns the formerly British White Star Line, and therefore the *Titanic*.)

One evening at the family's summer estate, strained relations between Henry and Tarr are bent past the breaking point when the latter catches the former in *flagrante delicto* with Nicole Linley, the live-in chaperone and companion to Tarr's wife Cornelia. Nicole also happens to be Tarr's live-in mistress and, as we later learn, a former J.P. Morgan moll as well. Henry's sack time with Nicole leads to a sacking by Tarr. During his departure he comes upon the aftermath of a mysterious murder, then briefly returns to Tarr's Fifth Avenue mansion, where he discovers documents implicating the millionaire in several corrupt schemes, including the one that bilked Lord Rutherford. This information is given to a *New York Times* reporter, who will search for corroborating evidence. The reporter in turn gives Henry a contact at White Star, which leads to a job as a wine steward on the *Oceanic*. Wine figures significantly in several effective scenes throughout the novel, no doubt a reflection of Aspler's authorship of several books on the subject.

Henry's career leads to a new love interest, Kitty Boyer, a stewardess whom he rescues from harassment with his pugilistic prowess. He also embarks on a persistent quest to amass further evidence against Tarr on both sides of the Atlantic. Henry and Kitty eventually seek and acquire a posting on the *Titanic*. By coincidence, Tarr and family are also destined to make this maiden voyage. They will be staying in the suite of J. P. Morgan, whose failure to make the trip, usually attributed to illness in historical accounts, is here linked to his conflict with Tarr. The final 200 pages use revealing details of the voyage as a backdrop for dramatic developments in the plot. Encounters and conversations are created between the lead characters and the Duff Gordons, Astors, Mollie Brown, and Benjamin Guggenheim. There is also a pivotal dinner scene at the captain's table, where Henry is forced to serve Tarr.

The shipboard intrigue includes some crucial wireless transmissions regarding Tarr's business practices as both Henry and antitrust legislators close in on him. Not surprisingly, a visit by Henry to the Marconi cabin includes a conversation about the nature of the medium with one of the operators, Harold Bride. Another conversation of interest takes place between Lightholler and Captain Smith over the possibility of an encounter with ice. The exchange discusses such things as how the lack of wind-induced ripples breaking against the base of an iceberg might make a potential sighting difficult; and how this situation could be compounded if the blue side of such an obstacle were to face the ship. Aspler probably drew this information from testimony given by Lightholler at the American Senate Inquiry. It indicates the thoroughness of his research, and helps make the dramatization more informative for those not familiar with the details of the disaster.

As might be expected, the climactic moments of the plot and the fate of the *Titanic* run parallel courses. What happens to some of the fictional characters also reflects the fates of several of the actual passengers. My favorite line in the novel comes from this section: as chaos engulfs everyone, Tarr, defiant to the

end, snarls, "I pay a fortune for this and the goddamned ship sinks." Less hu-
morous is a sexual encounter with murderous results, reminiscent of the one
that occurs at the same point in Robert Prechtl's novel.

Aspler's book seems not to have found a wide audience. The next *Titanic*
novel would. In 1991 Danielle Steel's *No Greater Love* was published. Unlike
Aspler's vision, Ms. Steel's is ensconced in the world of first-class passengers.
It is the story of Edwina Winfield, whose life is both shattered and then re-
made by the tragedy.

Twenty-year-old Edwina is the eldest child of Bertram Winfield, the self-
made publisher of a San Francisco newspaper and gentle and generous patri-
arch to a family of six children. Returning from England on the *Titanic,* the
Winfields, along with Edwina's betrothed, the dashing young Englishman
Charles Fitzgerald, are given a rude awakening shortly before midnight on 14
April. When accounts are reckoned the following day on the *Carpathia,* the
entourage has been whittled down to Edwina and her five younger siblings.
Her mission is clear almost immediately: to put her own life on hold and
manage the surviving brood to adulthood. In undertaking the challenge, she
becomes a quintessential Danielle Steel heroine, reflecting both the author's
name and image as suggested by the photograph on the back cover of the
book: someone who exudes feminine grace in conjunction with high-tensile
resolve.

The novel's first one hundred pages will appeal to anyone interested in
the disaster and unfamiliar with conventional accounts; the author has
done her homework. As real and fictional characters intermingle, so do
hard facts pertaining to the ship and the circumstances of the voyage. We
also have the ship turned into a veritable Edwardian loveboat—not sur-
prising, given Ms. Steel's wont and genre. Bertram and wife Kate have a
fulfilled marriage that keeps fulfilling itself. Edwina and Charles seem bent
on the same marital course. As both couples drift through the ship, they
encounter John Jacob Astor cooing with his young bride Madeleine, Benjamin Guggenheim appearing surreptitiously with his mistress, and Isodor
and Ida Straus, at the end of their natural lives, still inseparable as they face
this unnatural end.

The aftermath of the disaster takes Edwina from the U.S. Senate investigation through a life of noble self-sacrifice. The novel goes on to chronicle how
she keeps family and finances together and tries to reconcile this choice with
the possibility of romance and a more traditional life of her own.

To reveal the extended details of Edwina's life is unnecessary. Suffice it to
say that memories of the *Titanic* haunt the Winfields; the *Lusitania* makes a
cameo appearance; and there is a concluding segment where the once-fateful

voyage is retaken eleven years later on the *Titanic*'s sister ship the *Olympic*, with romantic implications. Throughout the novel, the changes wrought by the disaster on this single family serve as a reminder for what it actually did to numerous people who were on board and, psychologically, to an entire generation.

11

The Sinking in Cinema

The first major motion picture to be made about the *Titanic* never was. In 1938, David O. Selznick, with his magnum opus *Gone with the Wind* still in production, tried to lure Alfred Hitchcock from England to the United States to direct pictures for him. Foremost on Selznick's mind was a film version of the *Titanic*, to be based on the novel of the same name by Wilson Mizner and Carl Harbaugh. The book is a piece of pulp fiction that uses the ship as a backdrop for the story of a gangster renouncing his evil ways upon meeting the right woman. This kind of theme, the redemption of an immoral person, had become frequent in Hollywood at the time as a result of censorship policies imposed by the Hays office in 1934. Selznick envisioned a balanced production, part melodrama, part spectacle.

In retrospect, it seems obvious that this is not the kind of project that would have offered Hitchcock's directorial style the possibilities it thrived on—a psychological, rather than a romantic or technological, dénouement. According to his biographer, Donald Spoto, Hitchcock nevertheless endeavored to ingratiate himself to Selznick by claiming that he too, had entertained the idea of a picture about the *Titanic*, while his private conversations suggested otherwise. He mocked the limited possibilities of such a film, in one instance noting that a good way to shoot it would be to begin with a close-up of a rivet while the credits rolled, then to pan slowly back until after two hours the whole ship would fill the screen and *The End* would appear. Selznick had no inkling of this attitude, and as late as July announced that production would begin the following January. Hitchcock was quite flippant when interviewed about it, telling one reporter, "Oh, yes, I've had experience with icebergs. Don't forget I directed Madeleine Carrol."

Selznick was so serious about the project that he entertained the idea of buying the defunct liner, *Leviathan,* to use as a set. His plan called for the ship to be brought from New York to California via the Panama Canal and then be given a face lift to make her look like the *Titanic.* Plans for the film were eventually dropped or displaced by other projects. It has never been clear why, but we can easily surmise that with the world on the edge of a catastrophe—although some Hollywood moguls' concern centered on what Hitler's actions would do to their European movie distribution—filming an earlier one might be ill advised. (Fortunately for posterity, Hitchcock's first project for Selznick was *Rebecca,* which won a best-picture Oscar.)

Several years later, temporarily free from Selznick's constraints, Hitchcock did get a chance to make a film involving a maritime disaster. In *Lifeboat* (1944), he eschewed the possibility of filming the ship in the story actually sinking or using a cast of thousands. Instead, he created an intimate portrait of a handful of diverse survivors adrift in a sea of uncertainty after their ship had been torpedoed by a German U-boat. The film, although excellent, was intended to have value as war propaganda. Ironically, several critics at the time argued that this function backfired, because the German captain pulled aboard by the survivors was a bit too clever and complex. Creating a stereotypical villain would never be Hitchcock's style.

In the decades following the abandonment of a Selznick-Hitchcock *Titanic* film, four major motion pictures were made that deal at length with the voyage and sinking. The first is a 1943 German production, *Titanic;* the second, an American film of the same name released ten years later; third, the 1958 British film, *A Night to Remember;* and finally, *S.O.S. Titanic,* a 1979 American-British, made-for-television movie. Each of these efforts is more than competent, and one, *A Night to Remember,* is arguably a classic. As a minor theme, the disaster, either directly or by implication, has appeared in numerous films, from *Cavalcade* (1933) and *History is Made at Night* (1937), through the *Unsinkable Molly Brown* (1964), to *Time Bandits* (1981), and *Ghostbusters* II (1989).

Before assessing the four major films, it should be noted that they had precursors. Immediately after the disaster, newsreel footage was fabricated that used the *Olympic* to background the story, and at least one animated recreation also went into general release. A month after the sinking, silent-screen actress, Dorothy Gibson, starred in *Saved from the Titanic,* a quickie production of the Eclair Film Company. It was a case of art imitating life, since she had been a passenger on the ill-fated liner.

In 1929, British International Pictures cobbled together a low-budget effort at re-creating the tragedy. The film, *Atlantic,* was an early talkie and was released with English, French, and German soundtracks. A silent version was also available so the film could be exported to other countries and shown in theaters not equipped with sound-synchronized projection. Based on Ernest Raymond's play *The Berg, Atlantic* was a studio production, with the lifeboat scenes shot using a docked liner. The film did not have a successful run. According to Morduant Hall, who reviewed it in the *New York Times* on 6 October 1930, passable production values were overwhelmed by an atrocious and melodramatic script; a similar opinion has been expressed recently by film critic Tony Thomas. The credits reveal one notable name, Madeleine Carrol. I assume she did not play the iceberg.

If a major film about the *Titanic* was inappropriate for Anglo-American audiences in the tense prewar years, and unthinkable during them, Joseph Goebbels thought German audiences might be receptive to such a film; it could effectively couch anti-British propaganda in a lavish escapist spectacle. He recruited Herbert Selpin for the project, whose considerable and successful experience included three films in which maritime themes figured prominently.

Events surrounding the production of *Titanic* provided a drama as heartwrenching as the one depicted in the film. Two decades later, David Stewart Hull looked carefully at the full extent of what happened and n so doing interviewed Selpin's widow.

It seems that Selpin was initially enthusiastic about the project and the directorial challenge it would pose, despite being forced to collaborate with the hard-line propagandist screenwriter Walter Zerlett-Olfenius. Problems arose when Zerlett-Olfenius was sent to the port of Gotenhafen, now Gdynia, to gather background footage with the second-unit crew, while Selpin remained in Berlin filming the major scenes. Zerlett-Olfenius did nothing to expedite the films production, deferring instead to naval officers who were more interested in carousing than assisting the film crew, although they were obliged by the propaganda ministry to cooperate.

When Selpin found out, the incident compounded disagreements he had already had with his underling over the way the propaganda element was disrupting the artistic continuity of the film. The director went into a tirade, criticizing Zerlett-Olfenius's incompetence, his worshipful and deferential attitude toward the naval officers, and the officers themselves. Taking this as an insult to the Third Reich as well as himself, the outraged screenwriter went straight to the SS and the incident was brought to Goebbels's attention.

When summoned before Goebbels, Selpin did not recant. The enraged propaganda minister ordered the director arrested on a charge of treason.

Goebbels then found himself in a dilemma over what to do next. His previous meddling with the German film industry had led to a scandalous tragedy in which Joachim Gottschalk, one of the most popular matinée idols of the time, was badgered mercilessly to divorce his Jewish wife. He constantly refused, whereupon Goebbels ordered her deportation to the camps. Minutes before the Gestapo arrived, on 6 November 1941, Gottschalk killed his wife, their child, and himself. The German public was heartbroken, the film community outraged.

After pondering Selpin's case, Goebbels decided that the risk of further scandal must be overridden by the goals of the Reich. On 31 July 1942, Selpin was forced by prison guards to hang himself. The official cause of death was listed as suicide. Evidence confirming what many knew was murder surfaced in a 1947 trial. Zerlett-Olfenius was given a five-year prison sentence for his involvement in Selpin's death—a sentence that was never served; rumor had it that he escaped to Switzerland.

Titanic continued filming with Werner Klinger as director. There was tension on the set. Those involved in the production were tyrannized by a decree that Selpin's name could not be mentioned. When the film was finally completed, Goebbels faced another problem. Selpin's death was public knowledge, and the terror he had so effectively depicted on screen had now come to German shores with the start of allied bombings. A German release of the film was out of the question, but to recoup the enormous production costs, it premiered in Paris at the end of 1943 and had a short but successful run. Only after the war could Germans view the film, but British protests pulled it from distribution in the western zones, where it remained unavailable until the 1960s. East Germans had continuous access to the film, since the anti-British theme was ideologically correct and could also be interpreted as anti-capitalist.

Titanic is a fascinating mix: partly a lavish spectacle, partly a terror-filled docudrama. As real and fictional characters intermingle, generous liberties are taken with the historical facts. An arch-villain is created in the person of Bruce Ismay, who exudes evil in every scene in which he appears, and is costumed and filmed in a manner that recalls those dastardly villains of the silent screen who used to tie fair damsels to railroad tracks. In trying to save his corrupt company from bankruptcy, and to insure enormous profits, he bribes and coerces the captain to steam at full speed via the dangerous northern route so as to win the Blue Riband.

To give German film audiences the sense that they are not detached spectators to the events of the film, appropriate characters are introduced. A Teutonic first officer warns the captain about the questionable course the ship is taking and is duly chastised. The film also depicts the fate of German steerage passengers, who demonstrate more nobility in the crisis than the English of such birth. The most intriguing passenger, however, is a courtesan with a heart of gold played by Sybille Schmitz, who is ravishing in all her scenes. Her character, Sigrid Oole, is Danish and is cast as a brunette—almost but not quite of pure Teutonic stock. However, during the crisis her frivolous flirtations give way to courageous actions on behalf of the less fortunate, and suggest a bloodline that is part Valkyrie.

The film follows events beyond the sinking and rescue, to the British inquiry; it is the only Titanic picture to do so. The German officer, who made sure Ismay survived to be held accountable, is humiliated when Ismay's testimony transfers blame to the deceased captain. The officer's concluding monologue on who was culpable and why is unabashed propaganda and a technique that was occasionally employed in the finale of British and American pictures made during this era.

In the United States, a copy of the film can be viewed at the George Eastman House in Rochester, New York. Segments also turn up from time to time in television programs about the disaster. So effective is the depiction of the sinking in the film that fifteen years later parts of it were lifted (without credit) and spliced into *A Night to Remember*.

Little controversy would surround the next film called *Titanic*, released in 1953 by Twentieth Century Fox. In a sense, Selznick was right when fifteen years earlier he had championed the dramatic possibilities of such a picture. Unfortunately, his timing was off, and the opportunity would be realized by another producer, Charles Brackett.

The cautionary lesson of *Titanic* situated itself more comfortably in the postwar recovery years than it would have in the gloom-enshrouded late 1930s. The new mood was of optimism and promise, tempered by enough cold war tension to remind people that disaster might only be an air-raid siren's blast away. Another reason for Hollywood's interest in a *Titanic* film at this time was competition from television. Movie attendance was in decline; therefore the big screen had to offer what its competitor could not, and during much of the 1950s this meant grandiose spectacle.

Titanic—this title won out over *Nearer, My God To Thee* and *Passenger List*—was directed by Jean Negulesco, who would later regard the film as one of his best, and scripted by Charles Brackett, Walter Reisch, and Richard Breen. It premiered on the appropriate date of 14 April. The film won an Oscar for best original screen play, and had a renowned cast that included Barbara Stanwyck, Clifton Webb, and Robert Wagner. *Titanic* succeeds well as a period melodrama and is more than adequate in its depiction of the sinking.

The film uses the nautical events as a backdrop for the personal histories and aspirations of its main characters. (Exactly the reverse formula would be employed in *A Night to Remember,* made five years later.) *Titanic* is thus not so much the story of the ship as it is a glimpse of the stories on the ship.

The primary narrative centers on the marital breakup of Julia and Richard Sturgess, played by Barbara Stanwyck and Clifton Webb. After twenty years of marriage and two children, a daughter seventeen and a son thirteen, Julia realizes that differences in social class can never be overcome. When she married Richard she was a homespun girl from Michigan with basic American values. He swept her off her feet with his aristocratic charm and the era's equivalent of a jet-set lifestyle. As their children prepare to enter adulthood, Julia sees them becoming pampered snobs. Before it is too late, a withdrawal from caviar and a dose of apple pie is called for. She spirits them off to America on the *Titanic* without telling her husband. This scenario was partly inspired by the fate of the *Titanic* "orphans," Lolo and Momon Navratil, who were taken aboard by their father without his wife's knowledge. After he went down with the ship, they were returned to their mother in France.

Richard eventually finds out about Julia's plan and boards the ship in Cherbourg by purchasing the ticket of a Basque who is emigrating with his family—an unlikely scenario, since the voyage was far from being sold out. After depositing the steerage family (sans Papa) at the appropriate venue in the ship, he heads for first class to join his own brood, whereupon a war of wills ensues. Both children, he insists, must return with him on the next passage. The daughter, Annette, played with effective haughtiness by Audrey Dalton, will not have it otherwise. Julia concedes that battle, but will not let go of son Norman, played by Harper Carter with just the right blend of naiveté and exuberance. His performance missed earning an Oscar in the newly created children and animals category, losing out to Lassie.

To dissuade Richard, Julia unleashes a secret only she knows. The boy was not sired by him, but is the offspring of an encounter with an emotionally sympathetic stranger during an early estrangement in the marriage. Richard reacts to this by agreeing to support the boy financially but disavows all other involvement. His behavior toward Norman turns colder than the iceberg looming on the horizon.

These intrigues unfold amid elaborate sets and the comings and goings of the famous individuals now indelibly associated with the voyage—Astor, Straus, Widener, et al. For some reason, instead of Molly Brown there is a similar character played by Thelma Ritter, named Maud Young, who attributes her fortune to Montana lead mines, whereas it was Colorado silver in the case of Molly Brown. Several members of the crew also appear at regular intervals, among them Captain Smith (Brian Ahearne) and Lightholler (Edmond Purdom), but unlike *A Night to Remember* we find no Ismay or crew of the *Californian*.

Titanic avoids probing the various controversies surrounding the sinking, but it does try to provide a minimal overview of the events leading up to it. This intent is announced in the opening credits where, after a spectacular sequence simulating the formation of an iceberg, a notice appears claiming that the scenes of the crew navigating the ship are based on transcripts from the American and British inquiries. For most *Titanic* aficionados there are not enough such scenes, but they suffice to frame the primary melodrama. So do the special effects in the finale, although one suspects, from the movement of the actors, that the tilted deck is more the result of camera angle than set construction. In the print I screened there was also another "effects" anomaly: the ship is shown grazing the iceberg with the starboard side of her hull; the next shot, an underwater view, shows the reverse.

The film's primary course, however, is personal rather than nautical. It chronicles the way each member of the Sturgess family is changed by the voyage. Annette starts out with her nose higher in the air than the crow's nest. She rejects the advances of Gifford Rogers, a musically inclined student athlete from Purdue, wildly overplayed by Robert Wagner. He of course wins her over in due course, and she realizes that the best things in life are not necessarily a soirée at the Rothschilds and a titled husband.

Richard undergoes the most pronounced transformation, from charmingly arrogant to selflessly heroic, after he receives news of the plight of the ship from Captain Smith. Not only does he usher his family into a lifeboat, making amends to Norman en route, but he also delves into steerage to retrieve the Basque children and their mother. British audiences, nostalgic for a time when nobles were noble, must have appreciated this. Julia Sturgess does. She realizes that Richard has fiber in his being after all and that the marriage was worthwhile, even if tragedy must end it now.

The most interesting and unpredictable fate that befalls any character in the film occurs to Norman. He begins the voyage wearing short pants, then after several days argues convincingly for full-length trousers. He earns his new status legitimately in the concluding sequence, when he cedes his place in the lifeboat to a distraught woman and goes to find and help his father. They reaffirm their love and join in the singing of "Nearer, My God To Thee" as boilers explode and the ship goes under.

Several subplots play off against the primary story. The most effective one involves a priest (played by Richard Basehart) expelled from his order for alcoholism—an affliction induced by the pressures of serving a destitute parish.

In a moving encounter, distraught wife meets defrocked priest on deck the night before the sinking. The scene suggests the adulterous rendezvous fourteen years earlier that led to the conception of Norman, but this time the intimacy is spiritual and it is Julia who does the consoling. The exchange helps both characters shed their self-pity. When the crisis comes, the ex-priest ignores the "ex" and sacrifices his own life by going down in the hold to give counsel to the men trapped there. (Richard Basehart would go on to survive his next movie shipwreck as Ishmael in John Houston's *Moby Dick.*)

Titanic is a fine soaper. Contemporary audiences—now habituated to prime-time television variants of the genre, where adultery and the death of a child are no longer shocking themes—might be unimpressed. In the 1950s, however, nothing like it could appear on the small screen. As both spectacle and "adult" drama, it provided a worthy alternative to network fare.

One element used in the making of the film still endures, a twenty-eight foot, one-ton model of the ship that took the Sturgess family on their celluloid journey. It sits in front of the Maritime Museum in Fall River, Massachusetts.

For many people, among them British film producer William MacQuitty, *Titanic,* the movie, did not have enough *Titanic,* the ship, in it. The story begged to be retold, with the nautical events given center stage. A remarkable book facilitated this realization.

In 1955, a young advertising copywriter and part-time historian named Walter Lord (no relation to Captain Stanley Lord of the *Californian)* published *A Night to Remember,* a succinct 150-page account of the disaster. In the years since the immediate post-Titanic assessments of 1912 and 1913, no detailed re-examination had appeared. Lord did extensive archival research and wrote to and interviewed survivors. The book that emerged was an immediate success and created a surge of interest. This was partly a result of a readiness on the public's part to engage in some midcentury reflection and to look back at events that had defined the five previous decades. Television evidenced this trend with programs such as *The Twentieth Century* and its precursor, *You Are There,* both hosted by Walter Cronkite—the latter series even did an episode on the *Titanic.*

But the book's success owes more to Lord's literary skills than it does to the climate of cultural receptivity circa 1955. The text envelopes and interprets historical facts with a prose more typical of a compelling novel. Lord was one of the few, although certainly not the first, to write this way. The practice is far more common today and is sometimes characterized in literary circles as "postmodernist," one criterion for this label being the dissolution of boundaries between previously discrete literary categories, in this case documentary historiography and fiction.

Interest in Lord's book led to an adaptation for television in 1956. The broadcast, rarely mentioned in histories of the medium, is remembered today primarily by *Titanic* aficionados. Like its subject, it was both a milestone and a signpost for the end of an era. The program aired on *Kraft Television Theater,* a weekly anthology drama series on NBC—perhaps not coincidentally the network's doyen was David Sarnoff, whose rise to initial prominence was closely linked to his relay of wireless information about the *Titanic.* Direction was by George Roy Hill, who became better known as a film director during the 1970s. Noted actor Claude Rains provided the narration. With 100-plus actors and over two dozen sets, including water tanks and a stage made to incline, the production, which aired 25 March, was one of the most elaborate dramas ever broadcast live on American television.

During this era, known as the Golden Age of Television, experimentation was not uncommon. *A Night to Remember* was one that worked. It begged to be broadcast again, but since a restaging was out of the question for logistical and financial reasons, and videotaped productions would not be the norm until the next decade, a kinescope had to suffice. This was a version of the program filmed from a studio monitor rather than directly so as to faithfully record what the viewer saw. Fortunately, a video copy of the original kinescope now resides in the Museum of Television and Radio in New York City and is available for public viewing.

Before the term "docudrama" was coined, this program set a worthy standard for the genre. Claude Rain's commentary adds continuity and a wider sense of context, given the limited sets and visual options of a live broadcast. The acting is excellent, and the teleplay, adapted by George Roy Hill and John Wheaton, maximizes the possibilities of a small-screen live production. At times the makeshift and flimsy sets are obvious, but it must be remembered that the format entailed a different production each week; the challenge of creating the grand staircase, bridge, engine room, wireless cabin, and various spaces for each class of passenger on such short notice and with a 1950s television budget must have been a daunting one.

The ending, unlike those of previous and subsequent film versions of the story, avoids using the legendary *Titanic* anthem, "Nearer, My God To Thee." Instead, we get the Episcopal hymn "Autumn." The final plunge is not shown but is suggested in the closing sequence: Thomas Andrews, the *Titanic*'s builder, sits forlornly at a table in one of the lounges as the ship lists and crashing sounds are heard; the camera pans away from him and then back to what must have been a quick and clever replacement of the actor with a dummy, as a chandelier comes crashing down on the figure and the camera dissolves into a shot whereby the screen fills with water. Just prior to this finale, we get

a plug for the network and its head via the insert of a photograph of Wanamaker's Department Store, with the narrator telling us that during the sinking David Sarnoff was there, receiving the SOS.

This impressive telecast was one of the last of its kind. It aired from New
York at a time when the television industry was shifting its base to Los Angeles. Methods of production were also changing. At the time of *A Night to Remember,* the ratio of live telecast to the use of film for drama and comedy
programs was about fifty-fifty. By the end of the decade, the live format would
be completely superseded, leaving the medium with a creative legacy it has
rarely equaled in subsequent decades.

The same year *A Night to Remember* was televised, Belfast-born British film
producer William MacQuitty had a review of Lord's book brought to his attention by wife Betty. He saw in it a potential movie. The subject was dear to
him. At the age of six in 1911, he had witnessed the launch of the *Titanic.*
During World War II, as a maker of documentary films, he had pondered the
possibility of a movie about the sinking, but no specific strategy had come to
mind. Lord's book seemed to provide the necessary narrative. MacQuitty
quickly optioned the rights to it and gave the author a share in the film.

This did not go down well with his employer, the J. Arthur Rank Organization. They argued that such a film had already been done by Hollywood,
and that the story of the ship, as well as book titles, were public domain. Mac-
Quitty countered by noting how Lord had researched his subject for twenty
years and had created the kind of plot structure that was necessary for an effective film. Despite the prohibitive cost of such a project, he was persuasive
enough to get the go-ahead.

Roy Baker was hired to direct, Geoffrey Unsworth put in charge of pho-
tography, and Alexander Vetchinski served as artistic director. The task of
transforming Lord's text into a viable screenplay was given to Eric Ambler,
who, starting with *The Cruel Sea* (1953), developed such a feel for nautical
narrative that he went on to later script the *Wreck of the Mary Deare* (1959)
and *Mutiny on the Bounty* (1962).

MacQuitty also decided to shoot in black and white, using the screen's conventional aspect ratio, rather than in wide-screen Technicolor VistaVision, the
format of his previous film, the *Black Tent* (1957). This displeased the dis-
tributors, but it was the right aesthetic choice. Black and white, with its play
of light and shadow, has a dream-like quality that can evoke universality and
suspend disbelief more easily than color. This can impart a sense of timeless-
ness to a well-made historical drama, giving it a documentary quality—technicolor films, no matter how well shot or scripted, usually suggest the decade
in which they were made. Despite these contentions, I should nevertheless

note that in the 1953 film, *Titanic,* director Jean Negulesco's wished to shoot in color but financial constraints precluded this option.

Considerable credit for the film's enduring power must go to producer MacQuitty. However, to say it is his film goes against the grain of an influential and controversial strain of contemporary film criticism known as "*auteur* theory." It posits that a film is a work of art characterized by a certain style that results from the guiding hand of an author, or *auteur,* the director. This view arose as a counter to earlier notions that regarded movies as basically a collaborative form of mass entertainment, perhaps "art," perhaps not, at least not in the sense of a painting, novel, or symphony.

If one subscribes to the *auteur* theory—my own view is that the director's role, depending on the film, can hover between that of a conductor and a composer—then *A Night to Remember* is arguably a case of the producer as *auteur.* The unique look of the film, the choice of settings, and the decision to avoid major stars so as to background the characters and foreground the ship, were all MacQuitty's. He was on the set constantly, making sure everything was as authentic as possible. Walter Lord was brought over at MacQuitty's bequest for an advisory stint. He was impressed, as were several *Titanic* survivors who observed the production, Edith Russel and Lawrence Beesley being the most frequent visitors. Joseph Boxhall, the ship's fourth officer, was present throughout the shoot as a technical consultant.

Further authenticity was achieved when MacQuitty purchased from the *Franconia* some lifeboats that were similar to the *Titanic*'s. Finding a real ship's exterior to use for the crucial evacuation scenes proved more difficult, since various maritime administrator's were reluctant to have any of their vessels, even incognito, associated with the disaster. Luckily, MacQuitty was able to secure the partially demolished *Asturias,* which had her starboard side still intact. The film's interior scenes and model shots were done at Pinewood Studios, and the lifeboat sequences on Ruislip Reservoir. Conditions were cold throughout most of the filming. As a result, the cast's breaths and real shivering are visible, adding further accuracy to the look of the picture.

Although not considered an actor's picture, the leading player, Kenneth More as Second Officer Lightholler, would be associated with the role throughout his career; in 1960 he played the lead in *Sink the Bismarck.* Lawrence Naismith as Captain Smith was so true to character that the real captain's daughter was overcome by the resemblance when she visited the set. Among the other actors in the film, at least two have become better known since: David McCallum, who played wireless operator Harold Bride, can still be seen in syndicated reruns of his 1960s television series, *The Man From U.N.C.L.E.;* and Honor Blackman, cast as a concerned wife and mother in

first class, went on to be the original Emma Peel in *The Avengers* television series and Pussy Galore in *Goldfinger* (1964). Coincidentally, her costar in the
Avengers, Patrick Macnee, played *Titanic* builder Thomas Andrews in the television production of *A Night to Remember*.

A Night to Remember premiered in London on 3 July 1958, where it was a
critical and popular success, winning numerous awards. In the United States,
critical reaction was also favorable but public acceptance slower in coming because of the absence of major stars. MacQuitty spent a month doing radio and
press interviews in the States to drum up interest. The Rank Organization
brought over several *Titanic* survivors for the New York premier. The managing director of Rank, John Davis, thought it was a great film and wrote a letter to the producer so stating; he followed this with a decision not to renew
MacQuitty's contract.

In addition to its artistic merit, *A Night to Remember* is the first in a several-
decades long tradition of disaster film epics. It is clearly the best in the genre,
but has suffered subsequent critical neglect because of an association with
films such as *The Poseidon Adventure* (1962) and *The Towering Inferno* (1974).
As a British production, the film tends also to be ignored in historical and critical assessments of that nation's output because it does not fit into categories
that have typified her industry: the adaptation of literary classics, historical-
military epics, suspense-mystery thrillers, or social realist dramas. Hopefully,
with current interest in docudrama and its precursors now increasing in academic film studies, *A Night to Remember* will earn an appropriate reevaluation.

The docudrama nature of the film is obvious from the outset. Historical
footage of the launching is spliced to the dramatic re-creation of a christening
("creation" might be a more appropriate term, since White Star did not practice this ritual). This inaccuracy, and its depiction of the band playing the
now legendary *Titanic* anthem, "Nearer, My God To Thee," are the only
major clinkers in an otherwise accurate rendering. The opening scenes do de-
viate from Lord's book, but in less contentious ways, so as to help contextu-
alize what will follow. Instead of beginning on the ship, we see the
convergence of those who will make the trip: Lightholler traveling by train to
his posting while conversing about the *Titanic* with his wife, and passengers
in each class of accommodation making their way to Southampton by various means.

During the voyage, numerous stories are glimpsed but never told in full,
save the one pertaining to the ship. As we move through the thirty interior sets
built from the *Titanic*'s original plans, we glimpse passengers in each class engaged in various activities. The crew is observed serving them as well as tend-
ing the engines. But in this film, unlike the others, nautical updates are

frequent. Discussions on the bridge reveal the ship's course and the captain's expectations; scenes of the *Californian* appear early and warn of conditions ahead; and conversations in the wireless cabin allow us to eavesdrop on a center were information about both the vessel and the lives of the passengers converge.

Moving through numerous scenes is Lightholler. While Captain Smith, Bruce Ismay, and the ship's builder Thomas Andrews appear at regular intervals, Lightholler's scenes total more than all of theirs combined. He is the key figure in the film, serving almost as a narrator in character. It is an egoless role. Kenneth More plays "Lights" as the embodiment of an experienced seaman caught in unimaginable circumstances, one who responds with astute maritime instincts and unswerving reason. Lightholler is commanding, but not heroic in the conventional sense—he is instead a dispassionate and totally competent officer. This is not the kind of role that yields Oscar nominations. Nevertheless, More is nothing short of perfect, and one can readily understand why it was the most remembered performance of his career.

More than half of the two-hour production takes place after the collision. The action is relentless, but it is also meticulously paced. In all other *Titanic* films, and in most disaster epics, the climactic events take place in a rapidly compressed time frame. We accept this distortion as a convention of cinematic storytelling. In A *Night to Remember,* events follow one another in a way that is much closer to real time. Skillful editing and meticulous continuity make the format successful and contribute greatly to the emotional exhaustion that follows a screening of the film.

As the end of the ship nears, the camera goes back and forth between parts of her breaking up and the pandemonium among the passengers. The extras are convincing. So is the captain as he surveys the chaos and tries to orchestrate what must be done next. His reaction to the unresponsive ship in the distance (which the film, following the book, unequivocally assumes to be the *Californian*) is "God help you." This line is not in Lord's text, nor is a crewman's prefatory remark, "Bastard must be asleep." These scenes understandably outraged the *Californian*'s ex captain, Stanley Lord (who was eighty in 1958) and prompted further efforts to clear his name, a cause that is still being waged.

After the ship founders, attention turns to the scenario in the lifeboats. As the camera sweeps effectively from boat to boat and from one selected passenger to another, the issue of whether or not to save those dying in the water is debated. We hear only fragments of conversation, as befits the shattered world the survivors represent. Again Lightholler is the recurring presence, commanding an overturned boat and organizing the ragtag fleet. (To facilitate performing in those cold wet scenes, Kenneth More wore a wet suit under his uniform.)

The finale takes place aboard the *Carpathia* as she passes over the debris field left by the *Titanic*. We see a haunting recapitulation of what was so meaningful only hours before: the accoutrements of passengers in each class, musical instruments, unoccupied life jackets, and, lastly, all that remains to identify the ship: a life preserver with her name on it.

The next and most recent dramatic film to chronicle the voyage and sinking, *S.O.S. Titanic* (1979), was made expressly for television. Most movies made for the medium are hastily produced, minimally competent efforts that deal with a socially pressing problem—critics occasionally refer to the genre as the "disease-of-the-week-movie." When a more expensive historical theme is engaged, the format usually shifts to the miniseries, since the additional air time allows for more sponsor exposure and hence network revenues. *S.O.S. Titanic* is an exception. It is an expensive and historically detailed offering that was produced for a single evening's telecast, the *ABC Sunday Night Movie*.

The film is an American-British coproduction, more British in the production and more American in terms of the funding and the actors who get the most screen time. Billy Hale directed from a script written by James Costigan. Costigan spent a year researching the project, and his teleplay is largely based on accounts from the period. A major source was *The Loss of SS Titanic*, by Lawrence Beesley, played in the film by David Warner. Other notable cast members include David Janssen, Susan St. James, Helen Mirren, Ian Holm, and Cloris Leachman. Ms. Leachman, as Molly Brown, reprises a television role she played in 1957 on *Telephone Time*, a half-hour weekly drama series. Sometimes icebergs do strike twice in the same place.

Shooting took place in Long Beach, California, on the freshly repainted *Queen Mary*, Shepperton Studios in London; and in various parts of the North Atlantic. The broadcast did not draw the large audience hoped for, and, given the film's length (three hours with commercials), it has not been aired often in subsequent years. A video is now available, but it runs just 105 minutes. Interesting footage that adds to the mood, if not the story line of the film, has been deleted, and the opening and closing sequences have been altered. The original begins with an evocative and beautifully photographed scene of the *Carpathia* locating and taking on board the survivors, then flashes back to the start of the voyage, eventually rejoining the *Carpathia* in the finale. The video version puts all *Carpathia* footage at the end. The narrative sequence in the original cut is more effective.

S.O.S. Titanic strives to tell its story televisually and in a manner that avoids obvious overlap with earlier versions produced for the cinema. It is the first *Ti-*

tanic feature to employ color; the muted hues effectively tone the period decor and costumes. The script succeeds in presenting us with a panoply of interesting characters, whose lives we glimpse in both dramatic and undramatic moments. At times the camera seems to roam at random, stopping for the occasional voyeuristic glimpse. It could be something mundane, such as the making up of a room, or titillating, as in a deliciously wicked peek into the beauty salon in first class, a scene absent from the video. These conventions are staples of prime-time soap operas. Fluff to be sure, but well done. Details of the ship's navigation and the comportment of her officers were left to the precedent set by *A Night to Remember.*

Concepts used in the film may have also been inspired by the *Upstairs, Downstairs* television series (in which a major character perished on the *Titanic)* that aired on *Masterpiece Theater* during the 1970s. For example, we move back and forth between each category of accommodation. In first class, Astor (David Janssen in his last role) wonders whether his young bride loves him for himself or his bank account; in third class, Irish immigrants reflect on the New World, dance, and court; and in second-class, Lawrence Beesley (David Warner) and Lee Goodwin (Susan St. James) have an almost passionate attraction for each other. This couple is pivotal to the film, both in terms of their on-screen time and for the way they represent a generic middle class, observing and discussing the lives of those above and below their station. The two actors give an admirable performance.

The eventual collision sequence is more suggestive and less breathtaking than in the big-screen precursors, but is subtlely effective despite the budget constraints and reduced scale of a made-for-television production.

As the ship starts to founder, events center on the plights of the by-now familiar passengers rather than on the destruction of various parts of the vessel and the crew's reactions. The *Californian* incident is avoided; as noted earlier its depiction had resulted in *A Night to Remember* drawing criticism from her former captain, Stanley Lord, and his defenders. Both films, however, deal with the issue of the survival of the White Star Line's managing director Bruce Ismay, depicting him as somewhat calculating in an effort to abscond with his life. In *S.O.S. Titanic*, he surreptitiously enters a lifeboat as the captain watches disdainfully from the bridge.

With the ship in her death throes, the band plays, but they are not featured as prominently in those last moments as they are in other films, nor do we hear "Nearer, My God To Thee." Instead, the soft strains of "Rock of Ages" waft over the cacophony, providing an equally effective, though just as historically inaccurate, substitute. Elsewhere in the film the band is more noticeable. Period songs fill enough scenes to put the production on the edge of being a musical.

The concluding scene, as in *A Night to Remember*, takes place on the *Carpathia*. As Beesley looks out at floating debris from the wreck, he notes that we will never again look at the world in the same way. This echoes Lightholler's final words in the previous film, that the last vestige of certainty had collapsed.

More trenchant is the comment by Madeleine Astor (Beverly Ross), which constitutes the last line of dialogue. When told the tragedy was God's will, she responds, "God went down with the *Titanic*." This became a widespread blasphemy following the disaster, perhaps a corollary of the ship having been earlier declared a vessel that God himself could not sink. History had finally caught up with Nietzsche's philosophical pronouncement about the death of God voiced a generation earlier.

12

Resurrection

More than eighty years after the disaster, the *Titanic* is still frequently mentioned in the media. Recent discussions have centered on the *Californian* incident, the controversy over the salvaged artifacts, and the quality of steel used in the *Titanic*'s hull plates. Directly or indirectly, these concerns are an outgrowth of the most important moment in the history of the *Titanic* apart from her sinking: the discovery of the wreck in 1985. In the pages that follow, this event will be assessed, along with the context leading up to it and post-1985 developments.

In the two decades prior to the *Titanic*'s discovery, historical knowledge about her fate had been accumulating. In 1979, American psychologist/historian Wyn Craig Wade published *The Titanic: End of a Dream,* a meticulous study of the disaster and its context, emphasizing the American inquiry and the role of Senator William Alden Smith. That same year yielded the television docudrama, *S.O.S. Titanic.* What both events had in common, and shared with the successful 1985 expedition, was the assistance of the Titanic Historical Society, based in Indian Orchard, Massachusetts.

The THS has become the single most important chronicler of events and personages relating to the disaster. It was founded on 6 September 1963, a date chosen to commemorate the date in 1869 that saw the formation of the Oceanic Steam Navigation Company, Ltd., which would go on to develop White Star into a world-renowned shipping line. Today the THS boasts an international membership of over 5,000 and has become part of the very history it was formed to document. The organization was initially called the Titanic Enthusiasts of America, and started out with just six active (dues-paying) members and forty-five honor members, most of them *Titanic* survivors. The survivors were contacted through an "Information Book" compiled by a film distributor for theater managers who, when booking *A Night to Remember,* might want to get in touch with the survivors for publicity purposes. The book belonged to Edward Kamuda, son of a former theater manager and the person most responsible for launching the THS and navigating its successful course.

Kamuda had his initial interest in the *Titanic* disaster piqued by reading about it in high school. When the 1953 movie, *Titanic,* played at his father's theater, curiosity about the disaster was displaced by a passion to know as much about it as possible. Subsequent *Titanic* exposure in print, on television, and in film, convinced him that the memory of the event should be preserved, and toward that end the THS was established, along with an initial newsletter, *The Marconigram.* Funding came from the pockets of the active members, augmented by a modest donation from Walter Lord.

Eventually the newsletter, like the organization itself, underwent a name change. The Marconi Company was still in business during the 1960s and insisted that the use of their name was copyrighted; perhaps they also felt unease at being associated with the disaster. The publication was thus changed to *The Titanic Commutator*—often mistakenly referred to as *The Titanic Communicator,* notes Kamuda. A commutator is an instrument used to measure the degree of list on a ship, a device of some importance on board the *Titanic* after the collision. (It is also a term used in electrical engineering and mathematics, where it has different meanings, thus adding to the potential confusion of landlubbers.)

During its first several years, the THS received a modicum of recognition, and the newsletter became a lifeline connecting *Titanic* aficionados. Nevertheless, the enterprise remained small and marginal. On 17 September 1966, twenty-one members convened at the Seamen's Church Institute in New York for the first general meeting. The following year, with a total membership of fewer than 200, and few new subscribers on the horizon, it appeared the association and newsletter would go the way of the great ship whose legacy they preserved. If this was to be the case, the membership decided to bow out in spectacular fashion.

The April 1968 issue of the *Commutator* transformed the modest newsletter into an eighty-page glossy magazine featuring articles on the *Olympic* as well as the *Titanic.* Maritime organizations around the world took notice and the THS continued on course. In 1973, the tenth-anniversary convention, held in Greenwich, Connecticut, drew 140 attendees, 7 of whom were *Titanic* survivors, and attracted international press and television. Total membership soon exceeded 1,000.

In 1976, the THS presented a plan to locate and explore the *Britannic* (the *Titanic's* second sister ship, whose fate is discussed in chapter 2), along with relevant archival material that described what might be found, to Jacques Cousteau. He followed through on the project, accompanied by THS Vice President William Tantum.

Two years later, through the auspices of Tantum, the THS helped British television producer Alan Ravenscroft chronicle several ship disasters, among them the *Titanic* and the *Andrea Doria,* for his new series, *When Havoc Struck.* These collaborations prompted discussion of the possibility of locating and filming the *Titanic,* which in turn led Tantum and Ravenscroft into an association with Emory Kristoff of the National Geographic Society and Dr. Robert Ballard of the Woods Hole Oceanographic Institute. They formed Seaonics International and sought investors for the project. Tantum's death in 1980, however, scuttled the endeavor. Ballard did eventually succeed by other means, retaining the support of the THS, and in 1986 he deposited a plaque on the stern deck of the *Titanic* in memory of those who perished, which was dedicated to William Tantum.

The discovery of the *Titanic* has escalated interest in her fate and, as might be expected, membership in the THS. The society's conventions have become extravagant affairs. The 1995 version, held on the *Queen Mary* in Long Beach, California, attracted significant media attention. The *Commutator* too, has grown. It is now an impressive quarterly, devoted as much to the other great ships and their era as it is to the *Titanic*. The glimpses of social history the magazine provides are revealing and a boon to researchers. However, the level of documentation is somewhat less than those who are academically inclined might prefer.

The THS is still headquartered in Indian Orchard, Massachusetts, where Edward Kamuda operates the *Titanic* Museum out of the back of Henry's Jewelry Store, 208 Main Street. Across the street sits the long abandoned Grand Theater—like the *Titanic* herself, an ornate reminder of past dreams. It was here, in 1953, that Ed's father, Henry, showed the Twentieth Century Fox film, *Titanic,* to the local community. The collection of *Titanic* memorabilia housed in the THS's oversized closet of a museum is impressive. The term "cabinet of curios" came to mind during my visit—the label used to describe those compact exhibits of diverse artifacts popular during the Renaissance. The photographs, literature, and other material displayed combine to give the space the aura of a religious shrine.

More often than not, Ed can be found dividing his time between visitors to the museum and his work in the jewelry store. The man who perhaps knows more about the *Titanic* than anyone else, past or present, is soft-spoken and patient. The latter quality is a valuable asset in handling the numerous visitors, some of them casual tourists prone to asking the same, and sometimes inane, questions. In our age of hype and glory, it is refreshing to see such a sacred trust in so inauspicious a location, and to see it maintained with the understated grace that Ed demonstrates.

It is possible, of course, to surmise that if the THS did not exist, some similar organization would have probably emerged in the aftermath of the wreck's discovery. Indeed, several small ones have, but their history and commitment cannot match the original. It is a tribute to the foresight of Kamuda and the first coterie of active members that they initiated their project at a time when public fascination with the *Titanic* was subsiding after the diverse media interest generated in the 1950s by *A Night to Remember*. Recent decades have only served to vindicate their early insistence that the disaster was one of the defining moments of the twentieth century.

In 1976, with the THS-inspired exploration of the wreck of the *Britannic* prompting serious discussion of the possibility of doing the same with the *Titanic*, a remarkably prescient book appeared: *Raise the Titanic*. It was one of a series of action-adventure novels involving maritime themes written by Clive Cussler. Although the story was farfetched, the parts that dealt with the location of the wreck would shift from science fiction to scientific fact in fewer than ten years. Cussler's ability to forecast was not due to any mystic clairvoyance but to the result of a knowledge of undersea exploration and technologies, coupled with a sense of where they might be next headed. Before considering this novel, I should note that it is *not* the first case of art anticipating life with respect to the *Titanic*.

In 1898, in an extended short story called *Futility*, Morgan Robertson described the sinking of the largest ocean liner ever built, the *Titan*, which collided with an iceberg a few hundred miles from where the *Titanic* would later go down. Much has been made of *Futility* by devotees of psychic phenomenon. They often fail to mention that Robertson was a former seaman and a student of maritime developments who, in becoming a pulp fiction writer, applied that expertise to sea adventure stories; also overlooked is his denial, after the events of 1912, of any unique powers for predicting the future.

Futility's moralistic tone, implausible situations, and poor character development are somewhat offset by intriguing information about the ship and her fate. Comparing the *Titan* with the *Titanic*, respectively, in just a handful of categories, we get the following: 800 feet in length to 882 feet; 19 watertight compartments to 16; 45,000 tons to 46,328 tons; each voyage is in April; and both ships are triple screw, allegedly unsinkable, and capable of carrying 3,000 passengers, most of whom perish on the *Titan*.

Notable differences include the opposite direction of each ship's travel; foggy conditions in the case of the *Titan* versus clear in 1912; and the fictional ship not being on her maiden voyage. Robertson's behemoth also carried auxiliary sails, which leads me to suspect that the *Titan* was in some measure an embodiment of the promise and limitations of the *Great Eastern*, as well as a prediction of the design features that might characterize future ships.

Seventy-eight years later, in the novel *Raise the Titanic*, we also see an informed literary imagination creating futuristic vessels, but they move below rather than above the waves. What brings past and future together in Cussler's tale is a complex cold war saga that begins in Edwardian times. It involves a powerful radioactive substance, byzanium, with the potential of giving the nation that acquires it global dominance. Since the only byzanium remaining resides in a vault on the *Titanic*, the plot centers on a race between the U.S. and Russia to salvage, or as it turns out, to raise the ship.

To bring such an outlandish but successful action-adventure story to the big screen required both courage and foolhardiness. At $40 million in 1980, *Raise the Titanic*, the movie, became one of the top box-office disasters of all time. It cost and lost more money than the *Titanic* herself, which led British film magnate Lord Grade, who backed the venture, to allegedly reply, "Raise the *Titanic*! It would have been cheaper to lower the Atlantic." The film is badly scripted and largely miscast, a notable exception being Alec Guiness's brief but superb rendering of John Bigelow, a surviving *Titanic* crewman.

Jerry Jameson directed, with William Frye as producer and Martin Starger executive producer. The cast included Jason Robards, Richard Jordan, David Selby, and Anne Archer. Although universally panned, the film is not without its moments. The underwater footage is impressive, and the surfacing of the *Titanic* is one of the most spectacular salt-water sequences since the parting of the Red Sea in *The Ten Commandments*. It was done using a 55 foot, $5 million model ensconced in a $3 million, 10 million gallon tank, figures that would have doubtlessly impressed J.P. Morgan, since they alone exceeded the cost of building the *Titanic* herself. The large size of the model gives the look of the ship and her relationship to the water greater realism than is normally found in typical ship-in-distress effects sequences. Another impressive scene involves the *Titanic* being towed into New York harbor. John Barry's musical score is particularly evocative here, as it is throughout the film.

All speculation, fictional or otherwise, about raising the *Titanic* should have been laid to rest after she was discovered to be in two pieces with much of her structure collapsed. This fact, however, did not deter science fiction writer Arthur C. Clark. In his 1990 novel, *The Ghost from the Grand Banks*, he described an attempt to raise the stern section in the year 2012 and to tow it to Tokyo. Clark has had a long-term interest in the *Titanic,* and perhaps felt usurped when it was Cussler who managed to incorporate her into a science adventure novel. His own effort seems hastily written and falls below the imaginative standard of the typical Clark novel.

The real search for the *Titanic* had almost as much drama as these fictional accounts. It pitted a visionary scientist who tried to keep the media at arm's length, Dr. Robert Ballard, against eccentric oil entrepreneur and attention getter extraordinaire, Jack Grimm. The race also involved the rivalry between North America's two leading centers of oceanographic research: Woods Hole in Massachusetts (Ballard's affiliation) and Scripps Institute, in California, whose participation was made possible through Grimm's finances.

Although as a youngster Ballard was fascinated by the *Titanic*—hardly an exclusive club—he first gave thought to a more intimate encounter with the ship in 1973. As an aspiring marine geologist fresh out of the Navy, he began working at Woods Hole with the Alvin Group. *Alvin* was a three man submarine built in 1964 that had proven effective in dives of up to 6,000 feet. This depth limitation confined *Alvin's* use to the continental shelf and adjacent regions. After 1973, a modified titanium hull extended its range to 13,000 feet, which happens to be the approximate depth of the *Titanic.*

Ballard did not envision a search for the legendary ship as a singular project. Rather, it offered a chance to extend and test deep-sea search procedures, perhaps ultimately leading to a manned dive to the wreck. Oceanic research would be the major beneficiary, with information at those depths no longer limited to the sonar-driven abstract approach of the geophysicists. As a geologist, Ballard wanted to theorize about things he could actually see.

With the support of William Tantum of the THS, a viable *Titanic* search was planned. Woods Hole showed cautious interest, but a disaster at sea in 1978 involving the loss of expensive equipment being tested for the project led them to withdraw sponsorship. Ballard, Tantum, and the previous mentioned Seaonics International group then sought funding for the project. Jack Grimm briefly entered the picture as a possible backer, but his goals, which included salvage, were not consonant with those of Seaonics. When Tantum died in 1980, he did so believing Ballard would be the one who would eventually locate the *Titanic.* With the disbanding of Seaonics, Ballard became just as convinced that it would be someone else and reluctantly stepped to the sidelines while Grimm mounted three expeditions.

The flamboyant and confident Grimm attracted the participation of the Scripps Institute and the Lamont-Doherty Geological Observatory. We have no record of what scientists from these venerable institutions might have thought about his earlier expeditions to find Noah's Ark, the Loch Ness mon-

ster, and Tibet's Abominable Snowman. We do know that they took a d
view of the publicity he was generating for his *Titanic* project, especially t
incident involving a monkey named Titan. (Titan was named after the ship in
Morgan Robertson's story *Futility*, a literary work Grimm held in almost religious esteem.) According to William Hoffman, who would later chronicle the
second Grimm expedition (from the outset, Grimm sought to immortalize his
exploits in print and on film), the monkey was, at the appropriate moment,
supposed to point to a spot on the map where the *Titanic* would be found.
Not being primatologists, the scientists involved said, in effect, either the
monkey goes or we do, to which Grimm retorted, "Fire the scientists." San-
ity prevailed and the monkey remained ashore.

Guided by Grimm's historical knowledge, the first expedition took place in
July–August 1980. It employed a low-resolution sonar system, useful for de-
tecting large topographic features but lacking the sensitivity to make reason-
ably certain that a *Titanic*-sized object might be a ship. Bad weather
continually impeded the small research vessel, the *H. J. W. Fay*. Another set-
back involved the loss of the magnetometer, essential to identifying possible
targets as being metallic.

The second expedition, which took place aboard the *Gyre* in June–July
1981, tried to rectify some of the limitations of the first. Grimm did not believe that hype was one of those limitations; he amplified it in order to attract
more media attention and potential investors. With improved sonar, a magnetometer, and video and still cameras, success seemed considerably less than
a long shot. However, instead of using 1912 navigational information to rethink the possible location of the wreck, considerable time was spent revisit-
ing targets identified by the previous expedition's sonar. Each in turn was
eliminated in a frustrating countdown. When contractual obligations forced
the return of the ship, Grimm managed to finagle a few extra hours of search.
Using a video camera and microphone, but not the magnetometer, an image
was captured, accompanied by metallic sounds, of what appeared to be a large
ship's propeller. Grimm tried to convince the increasingly skeptical media that
it belonged to the *Titanic*, but many regarded the claim as another one of
what became known as "Grimm's Tales."

Nevertheless, he did convince backers to fund a third expedition, which
took place in July 1983 aboard the *Robert D. Conrad*. Despite an expanded
survey plan, the temptation to return to the propeller site again and again was
too much for Grimm to resist. With bad weather limiting the search, as it had
in the past, he was forced finally to abandon his quest.

Meanwhile, back at Woods Hole, Ballard continued his oceanographic research, most notably through the development of an underwater video unit,

Argo/Jason. Argo was a deep-towed vehicle for wide ocean-bottom scanning; *Jason,* a mobile robot on a cable-leash, was capable of peering into crevices and wrecks. The *Titanic* would become the unit's *Golden Fleece.* Funding was provided by the Office of Naval Research, which had a military interest in the technology. The office authorized a three-week test of the system to take place in the summer of 1985. Ballard had suggested the *Titanic* as a suitable target, but as far as the Navy was concerned, it was only an unofficial goal of the expedition. To increase chances of finding the wreck, Ballard used his connections to involve also IFREMER, the French National Institute of Oceanography.

The first part of the expedition started on 24 June when the IFREMER vessel, *Le Suroit,* left port to begin a sonar search, with any *Titanic*-like discovery to be later surveyed by *Jason/Argo.* After Ballard arrived at the operation, several more weeks of looking produced only elaborate data on where the *Titanic* probably was not located. When the *Le Suroit* part of the mission was over, the French sensed glory slipping away. Ballard had mixed emotions. He was frustrated by the elusiveness of the quarry, but relieved that he would have a chance to continue the search visually with his own equipment. On 12 August the torch was passed to the U.S. vessel, *Knorr.* She headed to a sector not covered earlier.

A key to finding the wreck, Ballard believed, was in trying to locate the debris field. In this kind of search, cameras have an advantage over sonar, since they are not limited to finding the main body of the ship. And so it was that shortly before 1 A.M., on 1 September, a boiler was sighted, which eventually led to the location of the wreck and those first memorable photographs.

Ballard's next challenge was to deal with the media. An inkling of how fast things were moving became apparent when he called Woods Hole with the news later that morning, and they already knew. So did the *London Observer,* which must have gone to press around the time the debris field was first spotted. They subsequently ran an inaccurate story claiming the wreck was being salvaged, an accusation that led to protests at the United Nations. IFREMER, already frustrated, became irate when the first pictures they saw of the wreck came from the American networks via satellite. Little did the French know that the American networks were miffed as well, since the first images shown publicly were via a Canadian network that had helped fund the expedition's documentation. In the midst of this maelstrom, an emotionally overcome Ballard was forced to break off one of his many radio interviews, with Tom Brokaw of NBC in this instance, when Ballard realized the *Knorr* was leaving the site before he had paid his last respects.

He returned to the site in July 1986 aboard the *Atlantis II,* with funding from the U.S. Navy and the support of Woods Hole but without IFREMER.

This time *Alvin,* the manned submersible, came along. Nine times Ballard visited the wreck, likening the experience to exploring the moon. The legacy of pictures taken attests to the epoch-making status of the project.

The knowledge, affection, and respect Ballard has shown toward the *Titanic,* as evidenced in his book *The Discovery of the Titanic,* articles, and media appearances, has continued unabated to the present. His wish has always been that the great ship be allowed to rest in peace. However, "wrest a piece" became the goal of the IFREMER-led next expedition.

Ignoring legislation passed with presidential approval by the U.S. Congress, which authorized the wreck site as an international memorial, IFREMER returned in 1987 under the protection of international salvage law. Funded by a consortium of American and European investors, their submersible, *Nautile,* scavenged an estimated 1,800 artifacts from the site. On one of the dives, William F. Buckley, Jr., was invited along, an experience he described in the 18 October 1987 issue of *The New York Times Magazine.*

Negative reaction to the salvage was immediate, especially from *Titanic* survivors and the descendants of those who perished. Most were not impressed by the offer made to them, of first choice of purchase of a selected number of artifacts. Even those with no emotional stake in the ship were angered when it became clear that the site had been treated carelessly. For example, the crow's nest was destroyed in an effort to recover the ship's bell, and no archaeological grid indicating the location of the finds seems to have been drafted, or at least made archivally available.

Further American reaction produced the Weicker Bill forbidding the sale or exhibition for profit of salvaged artifacts from the *Titanic.* Interestingly, one of its staunchest opponents was William F. Buckley, Jr., who, while not necessarily defending the salvage operation, did feel that what had been taken should not be denied access to an American market. The artifacts were displayed on American commercial television on 28 October 1988 in the show, "Return to the *Titanic* . . . Live!", which originated from Paris and is discussed more fully in chapter 1.

The French returned to the site in 1993 under contract to RMS Titanic, Inc., a New York–based company that planned a series of salvage visits to the wreck. The 1993 haul yielded 800-plus items, which were brought to Norfolk, Virginia, for sorting, thereby challenging the spirit, if not the letter, of the Weicker Bill. Strong opposition to this project was expressed by Robert Ballard and Edward Kamuda. RMS Titanic claimed that the pieces would not be sold off individually, and in 1994 they became part of a profit-making exhibit.

The exhibition, which was launched at the National Maritime Museum in Greenwich, England, has been controversial. It has also attracted legions of visitors and will soon travel, as did the Tut and Ramses shows a decade ago. Despite the questionable ethics of such a display, it provides an unusual and perhaps unprecedented glimpse of the material cultural remains of a ruin that dates from a period directly remembered by a handful of people still living.

An interesting offshoot of the discovery and salvage of the *Titanic* has been the possibility of establishing the near exact position of the ship when she sent her distress signals. This has important bearing on the *Californian* incident. Estimates of the *Californian's* position relative to the *Titanic* can now be undertaken with more certainty than was the case before the wreck was located. In his 1987 book *The Discovery of the Titanic,* Robert Ballard engaged the problem, thus fueling a controversy dating back to 1912; one that had already yielded several books.

Ballard's calculation of the likely position of two ships differs from the 1912 estimates, but the distance between the ships remains somewhere between the five and twenty-one miles minimum/maximum debated then. Those on board the *Titanic* claimed the former figure, believing, on the basis of the two inquiries, that the ship they sighted *was* the *Californian.* Captain Lord and his contemporary supporters (known as "Lordites") have favored the latter distance. If correct, this would mean that the mysterious ship observed by the *Californian* must have been a vessel other than the *Titanic.*

Other factors to consider include the *Titanic's* failure to respond to the *Californian's* Morse lamp, which would certainly have been visible if the two ships were as close as both inquiries claimed. Also, the ship sighted by the *Titanic* was later observed leaving the scene, while we know that the *Californian* drifted the entire night with her engines shut down. Again, the question of a third ship looms. The leading candidate is a Norwegian sealing vessel, the *Samsun.* Hunting illegally and not having wireless, she might have assumed the rockets were signaling her position to authorities, and therefore fled. It is also possible that a fourth ship was in the area as well, and that this vessel might have been the one the *Californian* unsuccessfully try to contact by Morse lamp.

These issues have been hotly debated in the 1990s and occasionally reported in both print and television news. The controversy led to a formal reinvestigation by the British Department of Transport's Marine Accident Investigation Branch (MAIB). Looking at the vast array of data, some of it conflicting, MAIB released its report on 2 April 1992.

The report is detailed and compassionate, but not conclusive. Respectful disagreements between investigators are forthrightly aired. One investigator believes the ships were five to seven miles apart and visible to each other, another contends it was probably seventeen to twenty miles, with mutual visibility unlikely. All agree that the *Californian* observed the *Titanic's* distress rockets and took no action. They also concur on what Captain Lord should have done: gone to the bridge, called the wireless operator to his post, and readied the engines.

The conclusion of the report contains a fascinating and convincing guess at what would have happened had Captain Lord responded to the first rocket and prepared his ship for a rescue effort. He would have immediately had to verify the *Titanic's* position, which, as the *Carpathia, Birma,* and decades of subsequent reassessment have shown, was about twelve miles east of her transmitted coordinates. Getting to the *Titanic* at night through an ice field would have precluded an all-out sprint. Under these circumstances, the estimated time of arrival would have been, at best, the time of the sinking, and more likely some minutes later. Little could have been done for those not already in lifeboats.

As a nonmaritime expert, I would add to the MAIB conclusion the following speculation: even if the *Californian* was the minimum distance and responded as rapidly as possible, thereby arriving, say, thirty minutes before the final plunge, what could she have done? Maneuvering into position to take up and then relaunch lifeboats would have been a time-consuming procedure, especially at night; in daylight, it took five to six hours of careful rescue work to get all survivors aboard the *Carpathia.* It would have also been time consuming for the *Californian's* crew to launch their ship's lifeboats and row them to the site. At best they might have been able to pull a few people from the water, at worst they would have faced a risk of being capsized in the confusion. Twenty-eight degree water, in any event, does not give those immersed in it more than a few minutes with which to help their own cause.

The 1992 MAIB report was not the only *Titanic*-related event to catch the public eye that year. In October, the IMAX film *Titanica* premiered in Ottawa, Canada. As of this writing the film is being shown in IMAX/OMNIMAX theaters located around the world and is already one of the most successful films in the twenty-five year history of IMAX.

Titanica is largely the brainchild of Canadian director/producer Stephen Low. He had originally wanted to film Robert Ballard's 1986 expedition using IMAX, but a combination of circumstances thwarted the plan: the lack of a second submersible to provide dramatic footage of the first approaching the wreck; the relatively primitive state of deep-sea lighting systems; and the ever-present difficulty of raising funds. These challenges were eventually surmounted and a new expedition took place in June/July 1991. Russia's Shirov Institute of Oceanology was invited and made available their research vessel, the *Akademic Kaldysh.* The expedition became a joint Canadian, Russian, and

American venture, committed to marine biological and geological research as well as to filming the *Titanic*.

As the first full-length IMAX feature, *Titanica* runs one hour and forty-five minutes, plus a fifteen-minute intermission. One of Low's goals was to make IMAX documentaries dramatically as well as visually appealing in order to attract the mainstream movie-going public. Contributing to the storyline are the crewmen of the *Akademic Kaldysh*, whose personalities we get to know as we follow them through their assigned tasks. Not leaving the dramatic aspect of the film to chance, important moments in the two Mir submersibles (one carrying an array of powerful lights) that were launched from the ship to explore the wreck were recreated in postproduction scenes shot in Toronto.

The film's deep-sea visual pyrotechnics are the result of a lighting system that generated the equivalent of 150,000 watts of illumination. Such panoramic lighting made navigating the submersibles less dangerous than in the past. Nevertheless, the venture was not without its hazards, since a bulb, imploding due to tremendous water pressure, could have fatal consequences by pulling the glass out of the portholes from the sudden pressure change. In all, thirteen dives were made, with the average time per dive being eighteen hours, most of it at temperatures near freezing; Low himself logged a total of forty hours undersea.

The underwater footage is breathtaking in detail and depth of field. The viewer is presented with many different parts of the screen to scan and dwell on. Shots of the debris field act as a prelude to finding the wreck and provide some of the most evocative moments in the film. A suitcase here, a shoe there, pieces of coal everywhere—the great ungluing of an era. We also glimpse a toilet, and are told they were made of iron for third class passengers, porcelain for second-class, and marble for first class. The suggestion is that each of these materials sinks in more or less the same way, as did the people who used them.

The film also has a human-interest side that centers on the multinational crew. Unfortunately, this aspect suffers because of the bias of IMAX, which is not a medium suited to personality depiction. The technical characteristics of IMAX result in an intense hyperreal quality that often renders the human face grotesque. IMAX works best when capturing a natural panorama or detail of technology. (Two years before the 1970 debut of the medium, Stanley Kubrick's *2001: A Space Odyssey* anticipated the style that would suit it. Scenes in *Titanica* of the Mir submersibles approaching the wreck are hauntingly reminiscent of Kubrick's great film.)

Nevertheless, IMAX technology is not without new dimensions to be explored. A successful one in *Titanica* is the use of 1912 still photographs to provide historical background. These images chronicle the building of the ship and the Southampton-Cherbourg-Queenstown leg of the voyage. Plate-glass negatives transposed to IMAX film provide stunning depth of field and a sense that the people in them are about to move.

At judicious moments between the narrative of the expedition and the archival flashbacks, we meet the grand dame of the *Titanic,* Eva Hart, who was seven when she boarded the ship. For most of the rest of her life she has been, and still is, a personable resource for those interested in the voyage. Fittingly, she closes the film. Speaking in a church with a vaulted ceiling that resembles the hull of an overturned ship, she tempers any excessive zeal we might feel toward the technology demonstrated in and by the film. We are reminded of what such an attitude led to in 1912, and are warned that history is not above repeating itself.

13

Conclusion:
The *Titanic* as Myth

In mid-May of 1987, I was in the Philippines traveling between Mindoro Island and Luzon Province in a small ferry. On December 21 of the same year, my memory of that passage turned from pleasant to haunting. At a Greenwich Village newsstand I picked up a copy of the *New York Times*. The headline told of a collision between the ferry, *Doña Paz,* and an oil tanker in waters I had once sailed; 1,500 were believed to have perished. I thought about that same casualty figure as it had appeared in a *Times*'s seventy-five years earlier. Later estimates would put the death toll at between 4,000 and 5,000.

Today the *Doña Paz* is largely forgotten, except in the Philippines, where litigation is still going on to compensate families affected by the tragedy. Without doubt, the fate of the *Doña Paz* has fallen victim to our short-term memory regarding third-world events. Yet, even the recent ferry disasters in Europe, which took hundreds of lives, have slipped from the recall of most of us. The *Titanic* is partly to blame. She wields the memory of her fate with a jealousy that tolerates no rivals.

Although we have learned much about the circumstances of her demise, a persistent enigma remains: Why is the tragedy still so meaningful to us? Historical facts alone cannot provide a convincing explanation. Indeed, the question itself defies closure, since the cultural circumstances in which meanings are produced and assessed constantly change. Nevertheless, the problem is worth addressing, even if the resulting answers must remain provisional and reflect a vantage point at the end of the twentieth century.

To say that the metaphoric implications of the *Titanic* disaster have given it the status of a modern myth is a contention that would probably gain acceptance among many cultural observers. But what do we mean by "myth," and how does the *Titanic* fit with our understanding of the term?

Certainly, the notion of myth as a fallacy, or inaccurate explanation for something, is inappropriate here. There is, however, another current usage of the term, which is applicable to historical events that have far-reaching implications. To illustrate it, we can use the example of a tragedy even more commented upon than the fate of the *Titanic*.

It is often said that the events surrounding the life and death of President John F. Kennedy have become a dominant myth in late twentieth-century American culture. Used in this sense, myth refers to events that represent more than the "facts" of history. It implies that the incidents referred to embody or help explain a wider set of values, beliefs, and aspirations. For example, a significant aspect of the "myth" of JFK is the notion that his death demarcates the end of a promising new direction for America; similarly, the *Titanic* disaster has often been referred to as the end of an era, or the end of a dream.

Although some commentators on Kennedy would agree with this "end of an era scenario," others have pointed out how the promise of a new America was fading, along with Kennedy's aura, even before the assassination—that Camelot was dying with a whimper before it ended with a bang. No matter. Debates such as this only add to the historical power of the event in question.

When historical events become the stuff of modern myths in this way, they reveal a way of thinking that is archaic and universal. All human cultures make sense of their existence in the world through stories, which, although not necessarily true in our literal sense, embody relevant knowledge and moral precepts at some level. For example, the oral myth told by the Maori of New Zealand to explain creation would probably not be regarded by us as factual, closer though it may be to Darwin's perspective than most premodern western interpretations. However, its literalness is not as important as its literariness: relevant insights about the natural world and Maori life emerge from and transcend the events recounted.

No less could be said of various works of literature in the western tradition. The book of Genesis, Sophocles's *Oedipus*, Shakespeare's *Hamlet*, and Melville's *Moby Dick* are rich in metaphor, archetype, and moral lessons. They are also variations on some aspect of the tragic, which gives them a certain relevance when mentioned in the context of the *Titanic*. Her demise is one of the most vivid cases in the history of western civilization of life reflecting art.

Assessing the mythic connotations of the *Titanic* disaster requires that we start by going beyond the event and consider the way it has been perceived and interpreted, as we have done in the preceding chapters. It is now time to take the next step and consider recurrent themes and symbols. One way to access them is to consider various traditions of myth interpretation and their applicability to events surrounding the *Titanic.*

Myths as a whole encompass such a wide range of phenomena that no one theory can succeed in explaining all their diverse forms and subject matter, despite the claims of practitioners. What makes the case of the *Titanic* so fascinating is that almost all major schools of myth interpretation seem to have something to offer.

If we take a sociological approach, even a non-Marxist one, class conflict emerges as a major element. The ship was a microcosm of the most profound disparities in wealth and status the era could yield. During the crisis, preferential treatment went to the wealthy in first class while many in steerage were held at bay. This situation reflected the Edwardian world view. Later commentaries would question its moral legitimacy.

This class hierarchy was, nevertheless, partly overturned by the course of events—a reversal of the natural order of things occurs frequently in myth. Despite their privilege, some notable doyens of the dollars perished. The oft-cited list includes Astor, Straus, Guggenheim, Widener, et al. This has become an enduring theme in subsequent tellings of the sinking, from "*Titanic* Toast" in African-American oral literature to Danielle Steel's recent novel *No Greater Love.* Perhaps over the decades those of us of lesser means continue to find solace in a situation where consummate affluence and extravagance—the Edwardian equivalent of "Lifestyles of the Rich and Famous"—was no assurance against Armageddon.

A psychoanalytical or psychological interpretation of the disaster would no doubt stress other elements. Freud's approach (he was fascinated by the real-life nightmare of the *Titanic,* but did not try to explain it) has a curious applicability. Playing fast and loose with it, we could say the *Titanic* disaster is a case of male culture being undone by female nature, a variation on the devouring female, or *vagina dentata* theme. Although ships are, of course, usually referred to as female (the reverse holds in French), they nonetheless represent an attempt by *Homo faber* (man the builder) to overcome the limits on his desire to conquer space imposed by the sea, the Great Mother of Waters. Add the sea's agency, an iceberg slicing away at this male creation (the "castration complex"), and the famous call "women and children first" (Nature saving her own), and the masculine is further jeopardized.

Silly? Perhaps. But-an-end-of-century ecological message can be culled from this interpretation. I will return to it in concluding.

In contrast to a Freudian approach, a Jungian one would perhaps see the *Titanic* disaster as a manifestation of humankind's overbearing urge to dominate nature. Unchecked reason and technology, Jung often argued, have created a dangerous split between the human and natural worlds that can render us vulnerable to disasters of our own making—the H-bomb was his primary example. Perhaps the *Titanic*'s fate, as myth, warns us of these tendencies, its effectiveness being dramatized by the ship's status as an archetypal vessel. This status suggests a symbolic womb capable of delivering a precious human cargo while being subject to suicidal tendencies that result from a false belief that nature has been mastered.

One of the most intriguing and recent approaches to myth interpretation derives from 'the intellectual tradition known as structuralism. Its most renowned proponent is French anthropologist Claude Lévi-Strauss, whose many volumes on primitive culture have sought to explain the universal working of the human mind that underlies all cultures. My own training as an anthropologist, during a time when structuralism was in vogue, leads me to suspect that the approach has some applicability to the story of the *Titanic* considered as myth.

Structuralism does not assume that the primary purpose of myth is to embody unconscious drives, desires, or symbolic archetypes. Myth works instead to mediate contradictions or oppositions relevant to the society in question. According to Lévi-Strauss, the formal mental operations through which myth making takes place derive from an unconscious pan-psychic capacity of the human species; however, the symbols used, and their meanings, emerge from social, cultural, and historical conditions. Each element in a myth ultimately relates to every other, not as part of a linear story but as a component in a communication system that poses and seeks to resolve a series of questions, many of which relate to the fundamental distinction between nature and culture.

Perhaps the approach can be made more comprehensible by applying rather than just discussing it. The first prerequisite of a structural analysis of myth is to draw out the episodes that make up the story. This enterprise is, of course, subject to the bias of the researcher and could be somewhat arbitrary. Nevertheless, taking the *Titanic* disaster and breaking it down into its familiar and persistent themes, we get the following:

1. Largest ship ever built embarks on her maiden voyage.

2. She accommodates all social classes and has state-of-the-art aesthetic and technological appointments.

3. Ignoring ice warnings, an attempt is made to set a speed record (the latter, although not true, is widely believed, therefore part of the myth).

4. There is a collision with an iceberg.

5. Women and children are given priority during sinking.

6. The rich and famous perish.

7. Nearby ship fails to come to the rescue.

Using a degree of imagination—critics of structuralism have argued that the approach is all imagination—we can posit that the central element on the list, number 4, is the important and pivotal one. It dramatizes the opposition between nature and culture. Numbers 1–3 assume the triumph of culture over the limitations of nature, and 5–7 dramatize the consequences of that assumption. The question as to whether culture can or should attempt to triumph over nature is thus answered in the negative.

Events in a myth, as Lévi-Strauss argues in his famous analysis of Sophocles's *Oedipus,* frequently involve the overrating of something and the underrating of something else. Applying this to our story, we can posit an overrating of size, speed, wealth. What might be construed as underrated are the natural elements of weather (that calm, clear conditions posed no danger) and climate (that the time of year and presence of ice were not an overwhelming concern). Perhaps we should also add maiden voyage, since they are normally cautious affairs tinged with superstition, attitudes ignored in this instance.

Other "structuralist" interpretations are possible, but it is unlikely they would stray far from the abiding opposition the *Titanic* disaste illustrates between nature and culture. If this is an underlying assumption at some level in all myths, as Lévi-Strauss claims, then the story of the *Titanic* brings it to the surface more unequivocally than almost any other story in the annals of western civilization.

Structuralism also posits that a given myth is often formally and thematically related to others, and that what is chronicled in one can occasionally be reversed in another. I would like to conclude by putting the story of the *Titanic* in this category. The sequence of events in it, rather than being totally unprecedented, can be seen as a transformation and reversal of what occurs in one of our most famous narratives: Noah's *Ark* in the book of Genesis. Both stories express moral precepts by recounting a disaster involving a great ship.

According to the account in Genesis, the *Ark* was built in response to a cataclysmic flood sent by God to punish a world guilty of excessive corruption, violence, and wickedness. God's original plan was to do away with the entire enterprise, but Noah prompted him to have second thoughts. Here was a man who, in resisting what others had succumbed to, walked in a state of grace and untarnished faith.

God informed Noah of the wrath to come and instructed him to build the *Ark* of gopher wood, 300 cubits in length, 30 cubits high, and 50 cubits wide.

The length of a biblical cubit has been estimated at between 18 and 36 inches. If, for the sake of poetic license, we take the latter figure and agree not to make too much of the comparison, the length of the *Ark* roughly equaled the *Titanic*'s 882 feet. Her height came close to the *Titanic*'s 97 feet from keel to boat deck. Noah's vessel, however, measured considerably broader in the beam than the *Titanic*'s 97 feet, since speed was not a high priority. God's oral blueprint also called for the *Ark* to have, like the *Titanic,* a three-tiered system of accommodations, although the *Bible* did not specify who or what went where.

Placing his faith in God and avoiding the excesses of the antediluvian era, Noah, along with his extended family and their menagerie, were spared. In the story of the *Titanic,* faith was placed in the conceits of the modern world— technology and inevitable progress. In yielding to their excesses, the ship perished.

Overweening pride, condemned in the *Bible* and in Greek tragedy (where it was labeled hubris), was the *Titanic*'s undoing. The resulting "nautical fall" recalls an earlier one in literature, whereby Captain Ahab's obsession with a white whale destroyed the *Pequod* in Melville's *Moby Dick*. And, as a case of reach exceeding grasp, the *Titanic*'s lesson appears to have been repeated less than six months after her remains were found, when the promise of the *Challenger* was immolated in January 1986.

What makes a comparison between the *Ark* and the *Titanic* so intriguing is how each vessel encapsulated the world of her day. Noah brought on board animals, crops, and a small coterie of relatives—a starter kit to rebuild civilization. The *Titanic* had impressive trappings that included a swimming pool, band, period staterooms, lavish dining areas, a café Parisien, gymnasium, squash courts, and ornate decor, all contained within a state-of-the-art, high-tech package. She was partly a grand hotel, partly a traveling exposition recalling the influential one held in Paris in 1900. In the jargon of contemporary pop culture, we could describe her as a floating theme park, part *Love Boat,* part *Fantasy Island.*

The theme of a self-sufficient world borne in the womb of a ship is a compelling one. In literature we find a renowned example in the *Nautilus,* the submarine created by Jules Verne in two of his novels, *Twenty-Thousand Leagues Under the Sea* and *The Mysterious Island.* Her captain, Nemo, is a technological wizard but also a connoisseur of high culture, especially art and music. Railing at the world for its excessive greed, intolerance, and violence, he creates an alternative one of his own. Eventually he succumbs to some of the very traits he despises and the *Nautilus* is destroyed; she gets resurrected in the second novel, only to go down for a final time. The idea for such an extraordinary vessel did not spring exclusively from Verne's imagination. In 1867 he was a New York–bound passenger on the maiden voyage of a refitted *Great Eastern,* perhaps the most ambitious sea vessel of all time.

Like the *Nautilus* and, from more recent genres of fiction, *Star Trek's Enterprise,* the *Titanic* has an aura of science fiction about her. She took part of the bounty of Earth on a voyage that often seemed more imaginary than real. The trip dramatized how the limits of human achievement could be overridden by arrogance and vulnerability.

A key to understanding our enduring fascination with the outcome of that infamous maiden voyage can be found, I believe, in an observation made by several survivors in lifeboats who watched the ship's terrifying last moments. They described the scenario as "like the end of the world."

Although we tend to think of that moment as more akin to the end of an era, the way it still haunts us suggests more. Amid recent news stories of the growing crises in our biosphere resulting from our disregard for nature, and examples of technology gone awry, is a continuing interest in the *Titanic* disaster. Could not the possible destiny of our planet, "Space-Ship Earth," as Buckminster Fuller used to call it, be linked in some way to the fate of the great liner? Have not the events of April 1912 now become a global metaphor?

In Genesis, the biblical *Ark* rescued part of an ancient world from a disaster invoked by God. The *Titanic* has become an *Ark* more appropriate to the contemporary world, her fate urging us to prudence with a cautionary lesson. She warns of a possible second deluge, this one of our own making, from which no vessel can deliver us.

Appendixes

THE CONVERGENCE OF THE TWAIN
(Lines on the loss of the "Titanic")
Thomas Hardy

I

IN a solitude of the sea
Deep from human vanity,
And the Pride of Life that planned her, stilly
        couches she.

II

Steel chambers, late the pyres
Of her salamandrine fires,
Cold currents thrid, and turn to rhythmic tidal
        lyres.

III

Over the mirrors meant
To glass the opulent
The sea-worm crawls—grotesque, slimed, dumb,
        indifferent.

IV

Jewels in Joy designed
To ravish the sensuous mind

From the *Selected Poems of Thomas Hardy* (London: Macmillan, 1916), pp. 119–21.

Lie lightless, all their sparkles bleared and black
        and blind.

V

Dim moon-eyed fishes near
Gaze at the gilded gear
And query: "What does this vainglorious
        down here?" . . .

VI

Well: while was fashioning
This creature of cleaving wing,
The Immanent Will that stirs and urges every-
        thing

VII

Prepared a sinister mate
For her—so gaily great—
A Shape of Ice, for the time far and dissociate.

VIII

And as the smart ship grew
In stature, grace, and hue,
In shadowy silent distance grew the Iceberg too.

IX

Alien they seemed to be:
No mortal eye could see
The intimate welding of their later history.

X

Or sign that they were bent
By paths coincident
On being anon twin halves of one august event,

XI

Till the Spinner of the Years
Said "Now!" And each one hears,
And consummation comes, and jars two hemi-
        spheres.

THE TITANIC
(Also known as IT WAS SAD WHEN THE GREAT SHIP WENT DOWN)

1 O they built the ship Titanic to sail the ocean blue
   And they thought they had a ship that the water would never leak through,
   But the Lord Almighty's hand knew this ship would never stand.
   > *It was sad when that great ship went down.*
   > *It was sad, it was sad,*
   > *It was sad when that great ship went down.*
   > *Husbands and wives, little children lost their lives.*
   > *It was sad when that great ship went down.*

2 O they sailed from England and were almost to the shore,
   When the rich refused to associate with the poor,
   so they put them down below, where they were the first to go.
   > *(Chorus)*

3 The Titanic left the harbour at a rapid speed.
   She was carrying everything that the peoples need.
   She sailed six hundred miles away, met an iceberg on her way.
   > *(Chorus)*

4 It was on a Monday morning just about four o'clock,
   When the ship Titanic felt that terrible shock.
   People began to scream and cry, sayin' "Lord, am I going to die?"
   > *(Chorus)*

5 The boat was full of sin and the sides about to burst,
   When the captain shouted, "A-women and children first."
   O the captain tried to wire, but the lines were all on fire.
   > *(Chorus)*

6 Now the ship began to settle and they all tried to flee,
   And the band it struck up, "Nearer My God to Thee,"
   And Death came ridin' by, sixteen hundred had to die.
   > *(Chorus)*

Adapted and arranged by Alan Lomax TRO-(c) Copyright 1964 (Renewed) Ludlow Music, Inc., New York, NY. Used by permission.

DE TITANIC
(As Sung by Leadbelly)

Captain Smith, when he got his load,
Might 'a' heared him holl'in', "All aboa'd!"
Cryin', "Fare thee, *Titanic,* fare thee well!"

Jack Johnson wanted to get on boa'd;
Captain Smith hollered, "I ain' haulin' no coal."
Cryin', "Fare thee, *Titanic,* fare thee well."

It was midnight on the sea,
Band playin', "Nearer My God to Thee."
Cryin', "Fare thee, *Titanic,* fare thee well."

Had them lifeboats aroun',
Savin' the women, lettin' the men go down.
Cryin', "Fare thee, *Titanic,* fare thee well."

When the women got out on the land,
Cryin', "Lawd, have mercy on my man."
Cryin', "Fare thee, *Titanic,* fare thee well."

Jack Johnson heard the mighty shock,
Might 'a' seen the black rascal doin' the Eagle Rock.
Cryin', "Fare thee, *Titanic,* fare thee well."

Black man oughta shout for joy,
Never lost a girl or either a boy.
Cryin', "Fare thee, *Titanic,* fare thee well."

Bibliography

PART I.   INTRODUCTION

Anderson, Roy. *White Star*. Prescott, Lancashire, UK: T. Stephenson, 1964.

Babcock, F. Lawrence. *Spanning the Atlantic*. New York: Knopf, 1931.

Brinnin, John Malcolm. *The Sway of the Grand Saloon*. New York: Delacorte, 1971.

Davie, Michael. *The Titanic: The Full Story of a Tragedy*. London: Grafton, 1987.

Dugan, James. *The Great Iron Ship*. London: Hamish Hamilton, 1955.

Dunn, Laurence. *Famous Liners of the Past Belfast Built*. London: Adlard Coles, 1964.

Eaton, John P., and Charles A. Haas. *Titanic: Triumph and Tragedy*. New York: Norton, 1986.

Emerson, George S. *S.S. Great Eastern*. London: David and Charles, 1980.

Guillet, Edwin C. *The Great Migration*. New York: Nelson, 1937.

Kirkaldy, Adam. *British Shipping: Its History, Organization, and Importance*. New York: Augustus M. Kelly, 1970.

Lightholler, Comdr. Charles Herbert. *Titanic and Other Ships*. London: Ivor Nicholson and Watson, 1935.

Lord, Walter. *A Night to Remember*. New York: Bantam, 1956.

Lynch, Don, and Ken Marschall. *Titanic: An Illustrated History*. Toronto: Madison, 1992.

McCaugen, Michael. *Steel Ships and Iron Men*. London: Friars Bush Press, 1989.

Marcus, Geoffrey. *The Maiden Voyage*. New York: Viking, 1969.

Maxtone-Graham, John. *The Only Way to Cross*. New York: Macmillan, 1972.

Pollard, Sydney, and Paul Robertson. *The British Shipbuilding Industry: 1870–1914*. Cambridge: Harvard University Press, 1993.

Robinson, Geoff, and Don Lynch. "The 'Unsinkable' Titanic as Advertised." *The Titanic Commutator* 6:4 (February–April 1993).

Tuchman, Barbara. *The Proud Tower*. New York: Bantam, 1986.
Wade, Wyn Craig. *The Titanic: End of a Dream*. New York: Penguin, 1986.

PART II.   WIRELESS WORLD

Aitken, Hugh. *Sytony and Spark—The Origins of Radio*. New York: Wiley, 1976.
Baarslag, Karl. *SOS to the Rescue*. New York: Oxford University Press, 1935.
Baker, W.J. *A History of the Marconi Company*. London: Methuen, 1970.
Booth, John, and Sean Coughlan. *Titanic: Signals of Disaster*. Westbury, Wiltshire, UK: White Star, 1993.
Brooks, Jennie. "The Wireless at Lands End Where the *Carpathia* First Talks." *The Titanic Commutator* 19:1 (May–July 1995).
Crowley, David, and Paul Heyer (eds). *Communication in History*. New York: Longman, 1995.
Douglas, Susan. *Inventing American Broadcasting*. Baltimore, MD: Johns Hopkins University Press, 1987.
Dreher, Carl. *Sarnoff: An American Success*. New York: Quadrangle, 1977.
Harrison, Leslie. *A Titanic Myth: The Californian Incident*. London: William Kimber, 1986.
Kern, Stephen. *The Culture of Time and Space: 1880–1918*. Cambridge: Harvard University Press, 1983.
Lepien, Ray. "The White Star Liner Republic (II), Part II Conclusion." *The Titanic Commutator* 19:1 (May–July 1995).
Lewis, Thomas. *Empire of the Air*. New York: Burlingame, 1991.
Lyons, Eugene. *David Sarnoff*. New York: Harper and Row, 1966.
Marconi, Degna. *My Father Marconi*. New York: McGraw-Hill, 1962.
Padfield, Peter. *The Titanic and the Californian*. London: Hodder and Stoughton, 1968.
Sarnoff, David. *Looking Ahead: The Papers of David Sarnoff*. New York: McGraw-Hill, 1968.

PART III.   CHASING THE STORY

Beesley, Lawrence. *The Loss of SS Titanic*. London: Heineman, 1912.
Berger, Meyer. *The Story of the New York Times*. New York: Simon and Schuster, 1951.
Davis, Elmer. *History of the New York Times*. St. Clair Shores, MI: Scholarly Press, 1971.
Emery, Michael, and Edwin Emery. *The Press and America*. Englewood Cliffs, NJ: Prentice-Hall, Inc., 1988.
Fine, Barnett. *A Giant of the Press: Carr Van Anda*. Oakland, California: Acme Books, 1968.
Gracie, Archibald. *The Truth About the Titanic*. New York: Kennerly, 1913.

Juergens, George. *Joseph Pulitzer and the New York World.* Princeton, NJ: Princeton University Press, 1966.

Kobre, Sidney. *The Development of American Journalism.* Dubuque, IA: Brown, 1969.

Lord, Walter. *The Night Lives On.* New York: William Morrow, 1986.

Mott, Frank Luther. *American Journalism.* New York: Macmillan, 1969.

Swanberg, W.A. *Citizen Hearst.* New York: Scribner's, 1961.

———. *Pulitzer.* New York: Scribner's, 1967.

Talese, Gay. *The Kingdom and the Power.* New York: World, 1969.

The Titanic Commutator. "Newspaper Headlines of the *Titanic* Disaster" 12:3 (1988).

U.S. Congress. Senate. *Loss of the Steamship "Titanic."* 62d Congress, 2d sess. Document 933 (1912).

PART IV.   DISASTER AS METAPHOR

Aspler, Tony. *Titanic: A Novel.* Toronto: Doubleday, 1989.

Ballard, Dr. Robert. "How We Found the *Titanic.*" *National Geographic* V. 168:6 (December 1985).

———. *The Discovery of the Titanic.* Toronto: Madison, 1987.

Barnes, Julian. *The History of the World in 10½ Chapters.* London: Cape, 1989.

Boles, Derek. "Catastrophe on Film." *The Titanic Commutator* 16:2. (August-October 1992).

Bright, Brenda. "*Titanic* on Film: Fact or Fiction." *The Titanic Commutator* 16:2 (August–October 1992).

Brown, Joanne Cullen. *A Journey into Thomas Hardy's Poetry.* London: Allison and Busby, 1989.

Buckley, William F., Jr. *Happy Days Were Here Again.* New York: Random House, 1993.

Clark, Arthur C. *The Ghost From the Grand Banks.* New York: Bantam, 1990.

Conrad, Joseph. *Notes on Life and Letters.* London: J.M. Dent and Sons, 1970.

Cussler, Clive. *Raise the Titanic.* New York: Pocket Books, 1988.

Dzwa, Sandra. *E. J. Pratt, The Evolutionary Vision.* Toronto: Copp Clark, 1974.

Finney, Jack. *From Time to Time.* New York: Simon & Schuster, 1995.

Gardiner, Martin. *The Wreck of the Titanic Foretold?* Buffalo, NY: Prometheus, 1986.

Gringell, Susan (ed.). *E. J. Pratt on His Life and Poetry.* Toronto: University of Toronto Press, 1993.

Hardy, Thomas. *Selected Poems of Thomas Hardy.* London: Macmillan, 1916.

Harrison, Leslie. "A *Titanic* Myth—Epilogue, the MAIB Report." *The Titanic Commutator* 16:3 (November 1992–January 1993).

Higham, Charles, and Joel Greenberg (eds.). *The Celluloid Muse: Hollywood Directors Speak.* New York: Signet, 1972.

Hoffman, William, and Jack Grimm. *The Search for the Titanic.* New York: Beaufort, 1982.

Hull, David Stewart. *Film in the Third Reich*. New York: Simon and Schuster, 1973.

Jackson, Bruce. "The *Titanic* Toast." In Levin 1972.

Jiwani, Yasmin. "Star Trek—The Voyages of Discovery: From 1942 to the Space Age." *CineAction* 33: 1944.

Kalman, Tanito. "Morgan Robertson's *Futility*." *The Titanic Commutator* 17:4 (February–April 1994).

Kamuda, Edward. "The *Titanic* Artifacts." *The Titanic Commutator* 17:4 (February–April 1994).

Levin, Harry (ed.). *Veins of Humor*. Cambridge: Harvard University Press, 1972.

Lomax, John A., and Alan Lomax (eds.). Negro Folk Songs as Sung by Leadbelly. New York: Macmillan, 1936.

MacQuitty, William. *A Life to Remember*. London: Quartet, 1991.

Mast, Gerald. *A Short History of the Movies*. New York: Macmillan, 1986.

Mills, Simon. *The Titanic in Pictures*. Buckinghamshire, UK: Wordsmith, 1995.

Pellegrino, Charles. *Her Name Titanic*. New York: McGraw-Hill, 1988.

Pratt, E.J. *Selected Poems*. Edited with an introduction, bibliography, and notes by Peter Buitenhuis. Toronto: Macmillan, 1968.

Prechtl, Robert. *Titanic*. New York: Dutton, 1940.

Robertson, Morgan. *Futility*. In Gardiner 1986.

Spoto, Donald. *The Dark Side of Genius*. Boston: Little Brown, 1983.

Steel, Danielle. *No Greater Love*. New York: Dell, 1991.

Sussman, Herbert L. *Victorians and the Machine*. Cambridge: Harvard University Press, 1968.

Thomas, Tony. *The Cinema of the Sea*. Jefferson, NC: McFarland, 1988.

Titanic Historical Society, Inc. *25th Anniversary Program*. September 1–4, 1988.

Wells, Henry W., and Karl F. Klink. *Edwin J. Pratt: The Man and His Poetry*. Toronto: Ryerson, 1947.

Whale, Derek. "Re-launching 'A *Titanic* Myth.' " *The Titanic Commutator* 16:3 (November 1992–January 1993).

Index

About the Author

PAUL HEYER is Professor of Communication at Simon Fraser University, Burnaby, British Columbia. His previous books include *Nature, Human Nature, and Society* (Greenwood, 1982) and *Communication and History* (Greenwood, 1988). He is co-editor of *Communication in History: Technology, Culture, and Society.*